A Man, A Woman, A Word of Love

A Man, A Woman, A Word of Love

JOSEPH S. PAGANO & AMY E. RICHTER

WIPF & STOCK · Eugene, Oregon

A MAN, A WOMAN, A WORD OF LOVE

Copyright © 2012 Joseph S. Pagano and Amy E. Richter. All rights reserved. Except for brief quotations in critical publications or reviews, no part of this book may be reproduced in any manner without prior written permission from the publisher. Write: Permissions, Wipf and Stock Publishers, 199 W. 8th Ave., Suite 3, Eugene, OR 97401.

Wipf & Stock
An Imprint of Wipf and Stock Publishers
199 W. 8th Ave., Suite 3
Eugene, OR 97401
www.wipfandstock.com

ISBN 13: 978-1-62032-372-4
Manufactured in the U.S.A.

All scripture quotations, unless otherwise indicated, are taken from the New Revised Standard Version Bible, copyright © 1989 National Council of the Churches of Christ in the United States of America. Used by permission. All rights reserved.

Dedicated to the parishes we have served:

Church of the Advent, Kennett Square, Pennsylvania
St. Chrysostom's Episcopal Church, Chicago, Illinois
St. Paul's Church, Milwaukee, Wisconsin
Emmanuel Episcopal Church, Baltimore, Maryland
St. Anne's Episcopal Church, Annapolis, Maryland

Contents

Foreword by the Rt. Rev. Eugene T. Sutton ix
Acknowledgments xi
Introduction xiii

1. **EXPECTANT LOVE—SERMONS FOR ADVENT 1**
   Spiritual Massage Therapy
   A New Way in the Wilderness
   Light into Darkness

2. **INCARNATE LOVE—SERMONS FOR CHRISTMAS 15**
   His Tremendousness
   A Christmas Prayer

3. **MANIFEST LOVE—SERMONS FOR EPIPHANY 23**
   Know Thyself
   Nothing Between Us
   A Good Cry
   Where the Beatitudes Make Sense
   Classroom Management
   What Happened at Church Today?

4. **REDEEMING LOVE—SERMONS FOR LENT 54**
   To Whom Do You Beautifully Belong?
   A Little Big Word
   Learning to See
   20/20 Vision

5. **TRIUMPHANT LOVE—SERMONS FOR EASTER 74**
   Let Him Easter in Us
   Set Free from the Stone

Contents

    6   Transforming Love—Sermons for the Sundays after Pentecost 83
              Bread of Life
              The Meaning of Pie and Other Holy Mysteries
              On the Border
              Being Like Jesus
              We're Number One
              Do You Love Me?

    Bibliography 109

Foreword

We must not think that our love has to be extraordinary. But we do need to love without getting tired. How does a lamp burn? Through the continuous input of small drops of oil. These drops are the small things of daily life: faithfulness, small words of kindness, a thought for others, our way of being quiet, of looking, of speaking, and of acting. They are the true drops of love that keep our lives and relationships burning like a lively flame.

—Mother Teresa

Our society seems to be in love with being in love. Popular songs, entertainment shows and literature are filled with words and images that try to convince us that happiness and self-fulfillment flows from the act of "falling in love"—as if it were something that we could catch if only we were lucky enough to be in the right place at the right time. In such a view, love can only be extraordinary, not a grace that is available to all—at any time and in any place—who are willing to accept its demands and responsibilities as well as its joys.

Amy Richter and Joseph Pagano are in love. Their collection of sermons about love in this volume is the result of their being in love, not only with one another, but with God and all of creation. These two Episcopal priests, both academicians as well as pastors, have taken vows to love one another in a lifelong commitment "until death do they part." They know, in the words of Henri Nouwen, that "love comes from a place within us where death cannot enter." They understand that love, in so many ways throughout history and in our own lives, has proven to be stronger than anything, even death.

Foreword

There was a song in a benefit concert some years ago composed in part by a long-term AIDS victim that contained these haunting words: "Love is all we have for now . . . what we don't have is time." Those words are true not only for those fighting a deadly disease; they are true for all of us. In a world suffering from economic crises, social dislocations and environmental degradation; in a world that knows too much hatred, conflict, poverty, hunger and brokenness, we are running out of time for solutions. We don't have time for divisions. We don't have time for personal hatreds and political wars. We don't have time for inter-religious conflicts. Love is all we have time for.

The sermons in this book bring a timely message of wholeness and hope for a world that so desperately needs healing. Joe and Amy are known as great preachers, but more importantly are known as a man and a woman who are filled with the love of God. The wisdom that they give us in these pages is the culmination of years of biblical scholarship, theological insight and personal experiences in their spiritual journeys that have led them to the depths of love.

May these pages open up the reader's heart to receive the heart of God, and may they release all of the love that can be found within.

Blessings and peace,
+Eugene
The Right Rev. Eugene Taylor Sutton
Bishop, Episcopal Diocese of Maryland

Acknowledgments

WE THANK OUR DIOCESAN bishop, the Right Rev. Eugene Taylor Sutton, with whom it is a pleasure to serve.

Thank you to our family, Mary and Stephen Pagano, Steve and Kristen Pagano, Rich Pagano and Christine Mackenzie, George and Pat Richter, June Richter, Andrew Richter and Jeni Prough, and Joel Richter.

We are grateful to the people who taught us at Harvard Divinity School; Princeton Theological Seminary, especially our preaching professor, Dr. James F. Kay; the General Theological Seminary; and Marquette University, especially our dissertation advisors, Rev. Philip J. Rossi, S. J., Dr. Deirdre Dempsey, and Dr. Andrei Orlov.

We thank the bishops with whom we have served, especially the Right Rev. Steven Miller and the Right Rev. John Rabb; the rectors with whom Amy served: Sharline Fulton, Dick Kirk, and W. Raymond Webster; and all the people in the parishes we have served who graciously listen and respond. Thanks to the leaders of these parishes, especially Suzy Brennan of St. Paul's, Milwaukee and St. Anne's senior wardens Sandy Criscimagna and Vollie Melson. Thank you to Bart Harvey of Emmanuel, Baltimore for a memorable retreat at Kanuga. Thanks also to the staff of St. Anne's Church: William Bell, Connie Saeger-Proctor, Kirsten Hair, Paula Waite, Rebecca Black, Wilbert Lee, Ben Mitchell, Ginny Hustvedt, Ernie Green, Carolene Winter, Jill Woodward, Laurie Hays, and Ken Kimble; and to Sarah Johnson, of Sermons that Work.

Thanks to Amy's writing group: Anne Brooks, Reid Buckley, Amanda Gibson, Roberta Watts, and our mentor, Laura Oliver; and to Christian Amondson and Tina Owens at Wipf and Stock, and Dr. Steve Fowl of Loyola University of Maryland.

Thanks also to the vestry and people of St. Anne's for having the courage to hire both of us to serve together as their priests.

Introduction

Beloved, let us love one another, because love is from God; everyone who loves is born of God and knows God. Whoever does not love does not know God, for God is love. God's love was revealed among us in this way: God sent his only Son into the world so that we might live through him. In this is love, not that we loved God but that he loved us and sent his Son to be the atoning sacrifice for our sins. Beloved, since God loved us so much, we also ought to love one another. No one has ever seen God; if we love one another, God lives in us, and his love is perfected in us.
—1 John 4:7–12

Our friend read this lesson at our wedding. We stood in front of Amy's father, a Lutheran minister, who officiated, and were flanked by our combined four brothers, two on each side, wearing suits and trying to stay cool on a humid August afternoon in Wisconsin. Our parents were there, along with more family members and friends.

Amy's grandfather, also a Lutheran minister, preached. He talked about knowing Amy since she was born, and that as a newborn she looked so self-satisfied that they called her the Little Pharisee. Grandpa then turned to Joe, looked him in the eye, and quoting Jeremiah, said, "And God knew you before you were knit together in your mother's womb." This scared Joe just a little. The look on Grandpa's face conveyed the message that it would be unbecoming for someone known by God since before his birth to cause any hurt to someone known by Grandpa since her birth.

Introduction

But Grandpa was also placing the two of us, and our intentions for love and faithfulness as a married couple, into the larger context of God's love and faithfulness. He was naming the fact that our small story—two young people who met at divinity school and fell in love and discerned a call into marriage—exists within God's great story of creation, redemption, and sanctification. No wonder it frightened us a bit.

We were married in August and we began seminary in September. Not everyone's idea of the ideal honeymoon, but it worked for us. We moved our few belongings into our apartment and began our married life together as students. We loved our studies so much we both completed PhDs—Amy in New Testament and Joe in Ethics. This has meant long days and nights learning languages and pouring over texts ancient and modern. But at the heart of our studies is our desire to know the God we love. Or, perhaps better, to know the God who first loved us. Consciously and unconsciously, our study of scripture and tradition has shaped our married lives.

Scholarship, as part of our vocation, is not just the accumulation of odd details, although each of us knows some pretty random stuff. Joe actually likes preaching on Trinity Sunday. We feel blessed by the ways theological insights inform and shape our understanding of the nature of God's love. It's hard not to sit up and take notice when Martin Luther describes the nature of God as "nothing but burning love and a glowing oven full of love."[1] There's nothing bland or pedestrian about this description. The love of this God is dangerous, transformative, enticing. To worship such a God is to risk being consumed, purified, set ablaze.

To preach about such a God is to be compelled to articulate the ferociousness of divine love: its ability to burn away any unnecessary or unholy thing the way a blast furnace refines iron from ore. It's also to articulate the consolation of a God who bestows grace and mercy on us like a mother who, at great risk to herself, will pursue her children who have wandered off in a storm, use her own body to warm them when she finds them, and bring them safely home. This God fires up the kiln so God can turn damp clay into a useful vessel, at no small discomfort to the clay, and calls us in from the cold and tells us to put our wet mittens on the radiator and come sit by the fire. This God is industrial and domestic, but never domesticated.

1. Martin Luther, *D. Martin Luther's Werke: Kriticshe Gesamtausgabe [WA]* (Weimar: H. Böhlau, 1883-), 36, 425.

Introduction

In the scriptures, we encounter a God who will stop at nothing to reach out to us, whose relentless love has no boundaries and who expects that we will do all in our power to follow God's lead.

In the book of Acts, we find ourselves swept up by the Spirit alongside the apostle Philip who suddenly finds himself plunked down on a road in the desert staring at an Ethiopian eunuch who is puzzling over a passage from Isaiah.[2]

"Watcha reading?" asks Philip.

"I have no idea," says the Eunuch. "But I want to understand. Can you help me?"

"As a matter of fact, I think I can." And Philip the Jew from Bethsaida climbs up into the chariot next to the Eunuch, a court official from Ethiopia, and proclaims the good news about Jesus to him. That is, he preaches to the Eunuch and in his sermon to this congregation of one, Philip describes Jesus. Jesus and the Eunuch have some things in common. Jesus was a man who had no descendants; the Eunuch has no descendants. Jesus was rejected; the Eunuch was rejected, most recently from worshipping in the temple at Jerusalem because of his "deformity." Jesus is someone who might understand the Eunuch, make him feel not so alone. But more, Jesus, according to the good news as Philip explains it, is interested in making a new family where everyone can be included.

"How can I join this family?" asks the Eunuch.

"Baptism," explains Philip. "That's with water, which is a shame, because we happen to be in a desert."

"Oh look!" cries the Eunuch, "Here's water in the wilderness!"

So Philip baptizes him, bringing the Eunuch into the family of Jesus. Then the Spirit whisks Philip away to his next preaching gig, while the Eunuch goes on his way rejoicing. He will never have a family by blood, but he will take the good news home to Ethiopia and bring new members into Christ's family where water is thicker than blood.

God still calls us to know the scriptures, to see Christ there, to interpret them through the lens of love, to translate them in such a way as to show how the stories of scripture really address the lives of people today. God still calls us to make new and unlikely friends in strange and unlikely places, and to keep our eyes peeled for streams of living water bubbling up where we least expect it.

---

2 Acts 8:26–39. The puzzling passage is Isaiah 53.

Introduction

As parish priests, we get to do lots of things. We lead Bible studies, teach confirmation class, fix leaky roofs, plan worship, recruit Sunday School teachers, balance budgets, pray with grieving families, prepare people for baptism, raise money, visit the sick, proofread bulletins, go to potlucks—all of which is important. But an anchor God sets to secure the vessel that is our faith community is the weekly proclamation of God's Word. Our week is shaped by preparation for this event. We study, pray, and listen for God's Word. We bring the joys and concerns of the parish to the texts for the week. We try as faithfully as we can to proclaim God's love for this community and the world. Week in and week out, in the words of scripture, and in the lives of the people who are our community, God's love challenges, provokes, comforts, exhorts, inspires, transforms, and nourishes.

The selection of scripture texts is not random. There is a lectionary cycle that follows the seasons of the church calendar, attuning us to the many dimensions of God's love. Like the facets of a gem, each season allows a different aspect of God's loving interaction with the world to catch light and shimmer. We are part of a larger body, the body of Christ, the church, and together as we move through the cycle of the seasons we are formed through worship and the scriptures we hear into the likeness of Christ. The discipline of living by a calendar larger than our own plans, appointments, and schedules reminds us that God's love is all-encompassing and continues to call us into a larger reality of love. We learn, again and again, and sometimes even in new ways, about the love of God through the yearly festivals commemorating the events of Jesus' life and the implications they have for his followers.

This is a book of sermons we have preached through the seasons of the church year. Each chapter focuses on a different aspect of God's love. In Advent, we look forward to the coming of Christ and the fulfillment of the promises of God. In this book, we call this Advent-informed love, *Expectant Love*. This is not wishful thinking at work, or mere optimism, but trust that God will keep God's promises, just as God always has, as attested throughout the narrative of scripture. The sermons in this chapter introduce us to repentance through massage therapists and tow-truck drivers, and God's light shining in dark places.

At Christmas, the festival of the birth of Jesus, the church celebrates the Incarnation, the coming of God as a human to experience the heights and depths of human life, and the coming of Christ in human hearts. In

Introduction

this book we use the name *Incarnate Love* to describe this festal season marking God's taking on human flesh to become Emmanuel, God-with-us. The sermons in this chapter focus on God's turning the world upside down by coming to us as a small child.

In Epiphany we celebrate the revelation of Christ to the whole world. The appointed texts for this season describe first-time revelations: to Gentiles, to his first disciples who hear the call and simply follow, to the congregation where he preaches. We call this chapter *Manifest Love* and the sermons focus on the revelation of Jesus as God's Son and as teacher of righteousness. We will hear about the sky being ripped open, the holiness of tears, and how Jesus manages someone screaming during his sermon.

Lent is when we contemplate the suffering and self-giving love of Christ. We call this season *Redemptive Love*. Our sermons focus on the costly love of Jesus who resisted temptation and went to the cross for us and for our salvation. We will meet sneaky serpents, tempters in the wilderness, and the blind who see.

Easter celebrates the resurrection. It is the triumph of life over death and the victory of God's love over hatred. We call this *Triumphant Love*. Our Easter sermons proclaim the resurrection of Jesus, being set free from stone, and the promise of new life available to us here and now.

In the Season after Pentecost, we are steeped in the stories of Jesus' life, his teachings and miracles, which provide the pattern for the Christian life, a life of forgiveness, healing, reconciliation, care, and compassion. We call this *Transforming Love* because through these stories we hope to be transformed into the people God calls us to be. In these sermons we meet excellent bakers, a persistent mother, ambitious disciples, and a forgiven sinner. In this and every season, God's love provokes and invites a response of love from us. *Beloved, let us love one another, because love is from God.*

God communicates through scripture, through the teaching of the church, through the Spirit moving through the community, and through the covenantal relationships into which God calls us. The two of us have taken a lot of vows: baptismal vows were made on our behalf when we were infants, and then reaffirmed by us as young adults; we made vows at our ordinations to the priesthood. In between, we made marriage vows to each other, in the presence of God and a gathered congregation.

We spoke words to each other meant to encompass all aspects of life: "for better for worse, for richer for poorer, in sickness and in health,

Introduction

to love and to cherish, until we are parted by death."[3] The vows begin with the grace we mentioned above: our stories are placed within God's story. The partners say to each other, "In the Name of God, I Joseph take you Amy . . ."; "In the Name of God, I Amy take you Joseph . . ." Gifts are acknowledged, given, and received, beginning with the gift of presuming to speak in the Name of God without being irreverent, blasphemous, or just plain foolish. But the gift is love, so speaking in the Name of God, who is Love, who is the source of Love, is fitting, even if daring. Speaking our names, *Joseph, Amy*, in the Name of God, acknowledges that we are all bound together. We have no love, know no love, comprehend no love, name no love, outside of God's love.

In binding ourselves to each other through marriage vows, we acknowledge Love's further gifts—the gift of two people, our histories, futures, and holy intention to live faithfully and fully until death comes and God has new ways for us to experience the fullness of divine Love.

In accordance with the Book of Common Prayer, we made our promises, gave and received rings as signs of those promises, and did what anyone having made such huge and comprehensive promises ought to do: we immediately knelt to pray.

The prayers focus not just on the newly married couple. They start with prayers for "the world you have made, and for which your Son gave his life,"[4] and they include prayers that "the bonds of our common humanity, by which all your children are united one to another and the living to the dead, may be so transformed by your grace, that your will may be done on earth as it is in heaven."[5] Once again, we find ourselves plunked down into Luther's "glowing oven full of love," our stories held within God's great story.

In between prayers for the entire world and everyone who has ever inhabited it, comes this petition, one of our favorites when we officiate at weddings: "Make their life together a sign of Christ's love to this sinful and broken world, that unity may overcome estrangement, forgiveness heal guilt, and joy conquer despair."[6] In other words, may this couple not be just two people held together by divine love. May they actually be-

---

3. *Book of Common Prayer*, 427.
4. Ibid., 429.
5. Ibid., 430.
6. Ibid., 429.

Introduction

come—serve as—living icons of hope. May the couple standing before us and before God—where we can see them, even if we can't gaze upon God directly—show us that Christ's love is so real, so powerful, and so effective that estrangement, guilt, and despair don't stand a chance against unity, forgiveness, and joy. "See!" we say, looking at the couple in their wedding garments standing before the altar, "right there in front of us—a sign! God is powerful, relentless, triumphant love." *No one has ever seen God; if we love one another, God lives in us, and his love is perfected in us.*

The sermons in this book are attempts to point to the love of God. Every chapter has sermons by each of us on the same scripture lessons—two takes on one text. Some of the sermons are joint efforts. All were given in the context of Sunday worship in a congregation we've served. They were written and preached by two people who are married to each other, who try to listen faithfully to God's Word in scripture and to proclaim what we hear to God's honor and glory and the service and up-building of God's community. We love each other; we love God; we love the communities with whom we serve. We hope these sermons will be useful to you and the communities you love and serve as well.

1

Expectant Love—Sermons for Advent

SECOND SUNDAY OF ADVENT, YEAR C

Luke 3:1–6

In the fifteenth year of the reign of Emperor Tiberius, when Pontius Pilate was governor of Judea, and Herod was ruler of Galilee, and his brother Philip ruler of the region of Ituraea and Trachonitis, and Lysanias ruler of Abilene, during the high-priesthood of Annas and Caiaphas, the word of God came to John son of Zechariah in the wilderness. He went into all the region around the Jordan, proclaiming a baptism of repentance for the forgiveness of sins, as it is written in the book of the words of the prophet Isaiah,

> *"The voice of one crying out in the wilderness:*
> *'Prepare the way of the Lord,*
> *make his paths straight.*
> *Every valley shall be filled,*
> *and every mountain and hill shall be made low,*
> *and the crooked shall be made straight,*
> *and the rough ways made smooth;*
> *and all flesh shall see the salvation of God.'"* (NRSV)

A Man, A Woman, A Word of Love

Spiritual Massage Therapy

JOSEPH S. PAGANO

A few years ago, for the first time in my life, I got a massage. Amy arranged this after a particularly stressful time at work. It was the beginning of the season of Advent, so at church we were gearing up for the holidays. I guess she thought a massage would help me relax and get into a better frame of mind as we prepared for Christmas.

Now, to tell the truth, getting a massage is not something I would have thought of on my own. As you may know, I grew up in New Jersey, and guys from my neighborhood don't get massages. Guys from my neighborhood get together to play pick-up basketball, get together to shoot some pool, or go out and get some pizza. I don't think "getting a massage" was part of the lexicon where I grew up. I can't imagine the amount of ribbing I would get if I told my friends that I couldn't hang out with them because I had an appointment to get a massage.

And yet that is precisely what I did a few years ago. And to be honest, I was a bit nervous. You know . . . a new experience . . . a complete stranger . . . taking off your clothes . . . getting a massage . . . I'm from New Jersey . . . you get the picture. But, I must say, I was greeted very warmly by a smiling, well-scrubbed, middle-aged woman, who said she was going to be my "massage therapist." I turned that phrase over in my mind . . . "massage therapist" . . . "massage therapy." It had an interesting, almost clinical ring to it. And it sounded a lot less threatening than the naked word "massage." "Massage therapy," I repeated to myself. *It couldn't be too bad. I could handle this.*

Then my message therapist told me to go into the room, to take off all of my clothes, to get under a sheet, and to lie face down on the table. And I got even more nervous. Disrobing and lying naked on a table in front of a perfect stranger, even modestly covered by a sheet, causes a little anxiety. But, I said to myself, "I'm a scholar, a theologian, and this is nothing that a little theology can't handle." *We are made in the image and likeness of God! We praise God because we are fearfully and wonderfully made! Our bodies are temples of the Holy Spirit!* "If this body is good enough for God," I told myself, "then it ought to be good enough for me as well." Theology to the rescue! Right?

Wrong! It didn't work. I was lying face down on a table covered only by a sheet. I felt naked and awkward and vulnerable. I felt exposed to the eyes of a complete stranger.

My massage therapist, who I must say was a complete professional, came in and got to work. At first, she seemed to be doing some exploratory work. She seemed to know how to find the places where my muscles were knotted and tense, places that I didn't even know were knotted and tense. "Not too bad," I thought. *Kind of nice. Sort of relaxing.*

But then, after this initial, exploratory phase, this nice, well-scrubbed, middle-aged woman somehow changed, and she began to hurt me. She dug her strong fingers into my knotted and stressed out muscles, and pain shot through my body. In a soothing voice she said things like, "it feels like you're a little tight here," and then she dug deeper into the knot. The pain was both excruciating and exquisite, and for the better part of an hour she subjected my stressed out and tensed body to massage therapy.

It is hard to describe this experience. First of all, it really did hurt. When she dug her fingers into a knotted muscle, pain seared through my body. But mixed in with this experience of pain, there was the deeper experience of my muscles loosening and becoming unknotted. So as I was lying there, with my lovely massage therapist boring into my muscles, I felt my body relaxing and being released from the grip of tensed and stressed out muscles. At the same time I was saying "ouch" from the pain, I was also experiencing sweet relief from my tortured and twisted muscle fibers. By the end of the massage, I felt wonderful. It was a painful process to endure, but in the end, my seized up and knotted muscles were relaxed and unknotted and I felt like a new person.

On her way out, my massage therapist told me to drink lots of water during the next twenty-four hours in order to flush out of my system the toxins released by the massage. My initial thought was, "Ick!" Decades of toxins released into my system. Not a pleasant thought. I must've drunk gallons of water that day!

In our Gospel lesson for this morning, we meet John the Baptist. And this morning I invite you to think of John as your spiritual massage therapist. John the Baptist was many things. He was a first-century apocalyptic Jew. He was the last of the Old Testament prophets. He was the forerunner of Christ. But today, on this Second Sunday of Advent, let's think of John as a spiritual massage therapist.

I say this because every year, at this time, the church in its wisdom requires us to confront John the Baptist, reminding us that Advent is not Christmas, but a time to prepare for Christmas. And every year, this meeting of John the Baptist in the wilderness catches us off guard. The Christmas decorations have begun to appear. People start getting those warm and fuzzy Christmas feelings. We dream of a white Christmas . . . the tinsel . . . the cookies . . . the eggnog . . . *The Nutcracker* . . . the giving and getting of gifts. And then, every year, John the Baptist interrupts our Christmas reveries by pouring a cold bucket of Jordan River water over our heads.

Traditionally, Advent is a time of penitence and self-examination, as well as a time of hope and expectation. It is a time to examine our lives, to acknowledge all the ways we fall short of the glory of God, and to try to clear out all the spiritual trash that is cluttering up our lives. The idea of Advent is that we are preparing for the coming of a very special guest. We are preparing for the coming of the Lord into our world and into our hearts. As John says, "Prepare the way of the Lord, make straight his paths."

To prepare the way of the Lord is a serious spiritual undertaking. Now, I don't want to be a Grinch. I like the tinsel and the trees and the carols as much as anyone. But there is a deeper meaning of Christmas, and Advent asks us to prepare for it. So in Advent we ask: How can we prepare the way of the Lord in our world and in our hearts today? If God is love, then what are those things that are keeping God's love at bay? If God's spirit is the spirit of truth and goodness and beauty, what are those things that mar God's spirit in the world? If God desires human beings to live in harmony and peace, then what are those things that keep frustrating these desires?

And when we ask these questions, there is John the Baptist waiting to greet us, saying, "Hello, I'm John, and I'll be your spiritual massage therapist. Take off your clothes, wade into the water, and feel yourself naked before the very eye of God. I'll be right in, and we'll get to work. And we've got a lot of work to do." And there are his rough, prophet's hands ready to dig into the twisted and knotted fibers in our spiritual lives. Under the Baptist's hands, we feel the pain of having the spiritual knots in our communal and individual lives identified and worked on. Has anger over some past injury got your soul in knots? Has malicious gossip torn the spiritual tissue that connects us one to another? Are you still nursing an old grudge against someone that is causing you to cramp up? Has consumerism got you feeling spiritually stressed out? Have fear and prejudice caused knots of hatred and intolerance to form in the body politic? The strong hands of the Baptist are ready to perform a deep-tissue massage on all the things that are blocking the coming of the Lord. It is a painful, but necessary process.

Yet, even in the midst of the pain, even in the midst of the searing in our souls, there is a sense that we are being relieved, released from the tensed and twisted fibers of our anger and our fear and our prejudice. As we undergo spiritual massage therapy, the toxins that were polluting our system are being flushed out in the waters of repentance. Every year, in Advent, we are invited to lie down on John the Baptist's spiritual massage table, and to undergo his treatment. It is painful. It really does hurt. But in the midst of it, we may find ourselves feeling like new men and new women.

This process of undergoing John the Baptist's spiritual massage therapy, a process of repentance for the forgiveness of sins, can make us feel slightly uncomfortable. Just raising the topics of sin and repentance makes some people feel uneasy these days. After all, aren't we living in an age of "I'm okay, and you're okay"? John the Baptist was decidedly not living in this age. John the Baptist thought more in terms of "I'm not okay, and neither are you." And it's precisely that kind of talk, talk of sin and repentance that makes us feel uncomfortable. But the really important question, the question the church puts to us every Advent, is not whether we feel comfortable with John the Baptist or not, but whether he is right or not. If I'm okay and you're okay, then we don't need to deal with John the Baptist. But if I'm not okay, and if you're not okay, then John the Baptist has a point. So the question we have to ask ourselves during this season of Advent is, are we okay?

Have you experienced any road rage lately? Do you find yourself harboring angry and hostile feelings toward certain people? Do you resent the achievements and success of others? Do you take a perverse pleasure in witnessing the downfall of others? Are there certain people you just can't stand to be around? Do you gossip? Are you still holding a grudge against somebody? Are you still feeling hurt and wounded by the insensitivity or maliciousness of another person? Are our corporate lives still plagued with violence, and poverty, and hatred?

Am I really okay? Are you really okay? Are we really okay?

If the answer is "no," then we may want to make an appointment with John the Baptist. Confessing our sins and turning away from them in a process of repentance may make us feel uncomfortable as we stand naked and exposed before the eye of God. In fact, confession and repentance can be painful as the tensed and twisted fibers in our souls are dug into and worked on. We may find the idea of flushing away the spiritual toxins in our system in the waters of repentance somewhat gross. But in the midst of this process of confession and repentance there is also a promise—the promise that through this process we are being made new creatures. We are dying to the old self, drowning the old Adam, so that we might arise a new creation, redeemed in the second Adam. Through confession and repentance we are being made ready to receive the greatest of all gifts, the greatest of all lives, the greatest of all loves, because the season of Advent is not only a time of self-examination and penitence, but is also a time of hope and expectation. It is, as John the Baptist reminds us, a way that we prepare for the coming of the Lord.

The promise of Advent is the promise that as we clear out the spiritual garbage in our lives, we are getting ready to experience once again the coming of God into our hearts. We remember in gratitude that God came among us, that God became one of us, in the birth of Christ in Bethlehem two thousand years ago. We look forward in hope and expectation to God's coming again to restore all things, to create a new heaven and new earth. And we prepare for the coming Lord into our lives in a new way this Christmas season, in a renewed birth of Christ in our hearts.

But before we kneel at the manger of the Christ child, and raise our voices with the angels on Christmas Eve, we need to wander out into the wilderness and confront John the Baptist, our spiritual massage therapist. His hands are strong and rough, the water is cold, and the table is bare. Are you going to keep your appointment this Advent?

A New Way in the Wilderness

Amy Richter

The Repentance Trip was how my family came to refer to one part of a summer vacation we took when I was in college and my two younger brothers were in high school. My family was traveling in a beige Pontiac J-2000 station wagon from Racine, Wisconsin westward. Our ultimate destination was Vancouver, British Columbia. Along the way we drove through the Badlands of South Dakota, saw Mount Rushmore, shopped for souvenirs at Wall Drug, and marveled at the multi-colored maize murals at the Corn Palace. We were following the route laid out for us on our AAA TripTik.

Do you remember the TripTik? It was a paper version of a custom-made map that came before Mapquest. Part paper map, part booklet, you unfolded the TripTik as you traveled. The TripTik—your personal TripTik revealed page after unfurling page of roads and travel information that started at your home, ended at your destination, and showed you all kinds of helpful information like tourist attractions and places to stay along the way. Our TripTik was our guide to adventure and discovery as it ushered us across North America.

"Adventure" and "discovery" took on new meaning somewhere north of the Canadian border. What our TripTik had indicated was a real road was, in fact, a potential road, an embryonic road, a road under construction.

It was late afternoon. We had been in the car for hours. We had drunk all the orange Fantas and eaten all the bologna sandwiches my parents had packed in the red Igloo cooler. My brothers and I had sung all the songs we knew and there was nothing but pre-hockey season talk on the two radio stations that came in clearly. We were ready to get to the lodge where my parents had made reservations, but we were still at least two hours away. Tall pine trees stretched high into the sky on both sides of the road. It wouldn't be too much longer before the sun would dip down behind the dense evergreen forest.

When we turned off the multi-lane highway onto the "road" indicated by the TripTik, we were greeted by a sign: *Proceed at Your Own Risk. Construction Ahead.* But the sign gave no information about how long the stretch of construction was or how far ahead. My parents exchanged glances. My father shrugged.

Just past the turn-off, the surface was paved, but there were no markings, no yellow stripes or lines to demarcate the shoulders. But there was blacktop—smooth and definitely drivable. So far, so good.

After a few miles, though, the asphalt gave way to gravel and a thin layer of tar. Dust from the gravel puffed up to the level of the open car windows. Bits of gravel pinged up against the undercarriage of the car as the tires crunched over the surface. The smell of the tar and my place sitting in the middle of my brothers in the backseat made me feel slightly nauseated.

"I feel sick," I said. My mother turned and shot me her best *don't even think about it* look.

"George, this doesn't look good," she said to my father.

"Check the glove box to see if we have a regular map," Dad replied.

"I'm really thirsty," my youngest brother said loudly enough to be heard over the noise of the gravel.

"And hungry," contributed my other brother.

"Roll up your windows! I hate the smell of gravel!" I complained.

"We have a ways to go," my father said. "Let's all be patient," he added, as he reached across my mom to rifle through through the glove box himself.

When the gravel ended and the road surface turned to dirt, my parents looked worried. Large orange grading machines were pulled off to the side of the road. No workers, or any other people at all, were in sight. We seemed to be completely alone. No cars were coming from the other direction. We hadn't passed anyone or been passed by anyone.

Worse yet, what at first seemed to be dirt was actually mud. We had come about twenty miles and it had taken some time to get this far.

My father decided to keep driving and hope that this was just a bad patch—that the "real" road, the passable road, was just ahead.

It was clear, though, that the car had begun to sink. The clinking of gravel against the car had given way to a slurping sound as the tires churned up mud and then were enveloped by it.

"We have to keep going," my father said, turning toward my mother. "If we can just keep moving forward, we'll be alright. We're way behind schedule, it's getting dark, and we're alone, but we'll be alright if we can just keep moving."

The mud deepened. The car became mired in the muck, sunk right up to the chassis. We could hear the mud and grit scraping against the wheel wells. We stopped moving.

My father gunned the engine, pretty much getting the result we all expected when we heard the sound. But he did it anyway, because it was something to do.

Dad turned the ignition off.

"What's happening, Dad?" my middle brother asked.

"Yeah, what's happening now?" my youngest brother echoed.

"Roll down your windows!" I demanded. "I need fresh air."

My father ran his hand over his forehead and up through his graying hair, like he did when he worked on the taxes. He sighed loudly.

After a moment of silence, he said, "Here are some options. We could treat this as a great adventure. But when it gets dark and cold and we're still stuck out here, that will grow thin. I could just blame the AAA people or the people who posted such a vague sign, but that wouldn't help and they weren't the ones driving. I wish I could take back my decision not to turn around at the first sign of trouble, but it's too late for that.

"I think we should all just sit quietly, look for birds before it gets too dark, and think of our best jokes to tell while we wait and hope that some help comes by." Mom patted Dad on the shoulder then pointed out a red-winged black bird. Dad ran his hand through his hair again and sighed.

Help came in the form of a tow truck with great big tires that travelled this particular stretch of road a couple times a day looking for people who don't pay attention to warning signs. The driver, wearing a red flannel shirt, denim coveralls, and high black rubber boots sunk almost knee-deep in the mud, said only "Enjoying your vacation?" as he waded up to the driver's side window and smiled in at my father.

We did get a new experience when we rode up in the extended cab with the driver as he towed our station wagon seventy five miles back in the direction from which we had come, reversing our course back through the mud, to the dirt, to the gravel, and finally to the wonderfully quiet stretch of blacktop. He towed us back to the main highway, then about seventy miles to the nearest garage.

We never made it to the lodge. We spent three nights in a roadside motel in the little town while we waited for the parts to arrive to repair the car. The time spent waiting gave my father the chance to buy a regular standard issue large rectangular paper map, and chart a new route towards Vancouver.

In time, we referred to that part of the vacation as *The Repentance Trip* because the arrival of the tow truck, its confirmation of our doomed attempts to move forward, and its pulling us back to safety embodied so well the definition of repentance—an active turning around, going a new direction, a change of heart, a change of mind, rather than continuing down the same path, moving in the same direction that is leading nowhere or somewhere dangerous, fast.

Repentance is not the same as remorse or regret. It is not listing all the ways things could have gone differently. It is not wishing you were a better person, that some things had never happened, that things like this wouldn't keep happening to you. It's not feeling guilty or ashamed. It's not something that leaves us stuck, or standing still, or spinning our wheels, going nowhere.

Repentance is about movement, letting yourself be grasped by God, reversing course, getting new bearings, and relying on God for directions.

The new life that follows repentance, the new direction that comes with a fresh start is what John was proclaiming in the wilderness. John's message is a call to action: repent, turn around, accept help. God is coming to meet you on a road in the wilderness.

Repentance can happen when you are confronted by something—maybe remorse, maybe disappointment or regret, maybe the sense that you are stuck, or sinking in the mud, and you're not sure how to get out. Maybe it comes from something as small as wishing you hadn't said something, or wishing you could take back something you did. Maybe it comes from something as large realizing that you have wandered off course into someplace dangerous and now that you're willing to ask for help, help may not be on its way anytime soon, and you decide that whether you have moments left or years stretching out in front of you, if you make it out alive, you want your life to count for something. You want whatever time you have to be something you can offer back to God. Maybe it comes when you realize there are other people with you on your journey and that your decisions affect them too and the wilderness is not a good place to be forever.

Repentance begins in many ways. When God meets us in the wilderness, on a way that is no way, or wherever we are headed in the wrong direction and offers us a way to get unstuck and move ahead with a new way of life, our best response is to accept the help and get on with the journey.

THIRD SUNDAY OF ADVENT, YEAR B

John 1:6–8

There was a man sent from God, whose name was John. He came as a witness to testify to the light, so that all might believe through him. He himself was not the light, but he came to testify to the light. (NRSV)

Light into Darkness

AMY RICHTER AND JOSEPH PAGANO

This is a dialogue sermon, with two voices alternating parts.
   Amy:
   During Advent, days become darker. Here in the northern hemisphere, nights literally get longer, light lessens, darkness descends. It's as if the creation itself accompanies us as we look for light to shine and dispel gloom and sadness. It is in these darkening days that a voice calls out to tell us of hope, of light shining in the darkness, a light no darkness can overcome.

   In today's Gospel we hear about a man who comes to bear witness to the light: John the Baptist, who was not the light, but came to testify to the light. John was sent by God to tell people who walk in darkness that God has not forgotten them. God sent John to tell people Jesus is the light of the world. The light of Christ is more powerful than darkness—than any darkness we might experience.

   God still sends John the Baptist to us on this Third Sunday of Advent, because darkness still descends, and we still need reminding that Jesus is the true light and Jesus the light of the world still shines into our darkness.

   Joe:
   I used to be a rather happy person. I laughed a lot and had a lot of friends. I enjoyed school, worked hard, got a good job. But lately it feels like I've lost my zest for life. I used to have goals I wanted to achieve: things I wanted to do, places I wanted to visit, people I wanted to see. But now, I'm not too sure what I want. It all seems rather pointless. It's not so much that work is a grind, as it is rather hum drum. It's not so much that people are mean, as it is they are rather irritating. It's not that I wouldn't like to take a course in photography or painting, as it is I'm just too tired to do anything about it. Not that I'm really doing all that much. I flip on the television. There is nothing on. I still sit and watch for hours. Night falls and the darkness overcomes me.

   I wished I cared more, but I just don't. Sometimes it feels as though all my family wants from me is the credit card or the keys to the car. How was your day? *Fine.* Anything new? *No.* See you later? *Don't wait up.* I'm not even sure people in my neighborhood know my name. I wave and smile when I pick up the mail or put out the trash, but it all feels rather phony. I go back inside and see if I got any messages. My sense of time seems all out of whack. Is it really December already? Wasn't it just August? How can the minutes pass so slowly and the months pass so quickly? I can't remember the last time I heard from an old friend, or talked to my aging aunts, or wrote a personal letter, or sat in the large easy chair I bought and read a good book. I can't believe it is getting dark so early these days. Better get ready for bed. Brush my teeth, set up the coffee for the morning, turn on the alarm, tuck in for the night and get ready for another day. I turn out the lights, pull up the covers, and pray in the darkness that I will be able to sleep tonight.

Amy:

Into darkness, light shines, even into the darkness of meaninglessness.

Jesus is the light of the world. His light shines on our path to bring courage and hope, direction, and purpose. In the words of scripture, we can hear Jesus say to us: Because God created you, because God loves you, every life has purpose. Every life has meaning. Every one matters. Including you. I am the Way, says Jesus. I will show you the joy of a life lived in service of others. I will show you the adventure of using your life to make a difference—even for those who may not notice or care, even for those who may not acknowledge or thank you. I know what that is like. I know.

Ask me what I want from you. Look at what I have given you to use for me—what I have equipped you with, empowered you for. Trust me. Rely on me for the courage to reach out beyond yourself. To reject the powers of darkness who tempt you to say, who cares? Why bother? Let my light shine on your path. Take my hand and let me walk beside you and watch as the darkness recedes.

I may not call you to something large or something the world will notice. I may call you to be faithful in small and steadfast ways. Trust that I am the Way. My light will dispel darkness and illumine your purpose and path.

Joe:

I saw the big letter D, written in red ink at the top of the page and I burst into tears. Admittedly, I was only seven years old. But I was in love with my teacher and I wanted her to love me. When I did well and she praised me, I felt wonderful.

I don't know why I did so poorly on the test, and, to tell the truth, I didn't really care whether I knew the answers or not. But I did care what Mrs. Johnson thought of me and now she must think me a very foolish little boy. Being clever was my way of saying I want you to love me. And what did I do? I earned a big fat D. I felt not only foolish, but rejected. It created a dark and hurt place in my little heart.

That wound and darkness has stayed with me. I grew up, of course, but all along I've desperately wanted people to love me. The popular kids when I was a teenager, the girl with curly hair and freckles in high school, my English professor in college, my mentor at work. If I did well, I'd get a pat on the back or a hug, and it felt like I earned an A+. I basked in the light of praise. But if I didn't, there was that big fat D . . . written in red ink . . . circled . . . underlined . . . twice. And I shrunk in the darkness of rejection.

Why do I say such stupid things and tell such stupid jokes? I haven't read the right books, I don't know a thing about wine, I don't live in the right neighborhood, and my golf game is rotten. I have found it easier to no longer risk the shame of rejection. I just keep to myself. And who knows maybe someday someone will ask me what I think, and I'll be clever and funny. Because I really do care what people think of me. I really do want them to love me. Like Mrs. Johnson, my second grade teacher. Who gave me a D and broke my heart.

Amy:

Into darkness, light shines, even into the darkness of rejection.

Jesus, Light of the world, says to us, I am the Truth. And the truth is you are loved with a perfect love, an unconditional love that you do not have to earn, merit, or deserve; a love that you cannot earn, or merit, or deserve. This perfect love is just a gift to you. It is a love you cannot lose.

People will disappoint you. You will disappoint people. If you are honest, you will disappoint yourself. People may reject you and it may hurt you deeply, especially if you long for their love. I know. I know. I am the Truth and the truth is you are loved more than you can ask or imagine.

Why do you let past hurts be the lens through which you see yourself? Why do you let an experience of rejection distort your vision? Why do you allow your past failure to be your only guide?

It is good to desire love. God is love. When you seek approval, what your heart of hearts is really seeking is the approval and love of God. And here is the truth: you already have it. You already have the love of God, the love that made all that is and ever shall be, the love that sent me into the world to show you perfect love. Live from that love—God's love—which already holds you close—live from that love so you can accept love, give love, show love, risk all for love. Trust my truth: Perfect love casts out fear. My light shines and even the darkness of rejection will not overcome it.

A Man, A Woman, A Word of Love

Joe:

When I got the news that he died, it felt like someone had kicked me in the gut. Massive heart attack, dead by the time the ambulance arrived, forty-four years old, two young kids, my favorite uncle. Wham, right in the stomach, knocking the breath out of me. I really couldn't breathe for a while, gasping for breath between sobs. But even after my breathing returned to normal, it still felt like I couldn't catch my breath. People's voices seemed muffled and far away. My vision seemed to tunnel, focusing only on something in the distance, all the rest fuzzing and graying around the edges. The darkness of grief closed in.

I was in a strange city far from the rest of my family. I wandered streets and alleyways oblivious to my surroundings. I returned to my dorm room and tried to find a book I was supposed to read. In a single, small room, I could not find where I put the stupid book. I began to cry because I couldn't find my book. I tried to read another book. I read the same sentence twenty times. I couldn't remember what I just read, so I read it again. I crawled into bed and slept. I woke up startled. At first I didn't know where I was. When I recognized my room, I sat up. I had no idea what time it was, whether it was day or night. I sat on my bed, alone and in the dark.

Amy:

Into darkness, light shines, even into the darkness of grief.

Jesus, Light of the world, says, I am the Life. God does not leave you alone in your grief. God does not abandon you in your sadness. God sent me into the world to bring Life. I did not stand aloof from sadness. I did not hover above sorrow. I wept at the death of my friend. I weep with you and for you in your pain and loss. But I know your tears will not be the end of the story. I know that death does not have the last word. I went through death and God raised me to life again. Death cannot extinguish the light of life and I have a prepared for you a dwelling place eternal in the heavens. Let your grief be a reminder that you have loved, that love abides. Let the brokenness you feel when you lose someone dear be a reminder that there is something more, a wholeness beyond this world, where you will be reunited with those you love but see no longer. Trust that I am the Life. My light shines, and even the darkness of grief will not overcome it.

Jesus—Light of the world, Way, Truth, Life—come, shine in our lives. Shine in our world. Dispel the darkness.

2

Incarnate Love—Sermons for Christmas

CHRISTMAS EVE

Luke 2:1–7

In those days a decree went out from Emperor Augustus that all the world should be registered. This was the first registration and was taken while Quirinius was governor of Syria. All went to their own towns to be registered. Joseph also went from the town of Nazareth in Galilee to Judea, to the city of David called Bethlehem, because he was descended from the house and family of David. He went to be registered with Mary, to whom he was engaged and who was expecting a child. While they were there, the time came for her to deliver her child. And she gave birth to her firstborn son and wrapped him in bands of cloth, and laid him in a manger, because there was no place for them in the inn. (NRSV)

A Man, A Woman, A Word of Love

His Tremendousness

Joseph S. Pagano

A couple of years ago, an obituary appeared in *The New York Times* about Giorgio Carbone, the elected prince of Seborga. It recounted the life and times and 46-year reign of Prince Giorgio the First. It was actually a rather charming story. Seborga is a small town in northwest Italy with a population of approximately 2,000 people. Italy sees Seborga as a commune in the province of Imperia. Giorgio Carbone, however, did not. In 1963, Carbone convinced his neighbors that Seborga was not part of the surrounding Italian nation, but was rather an ancient principality unlawfully denied its sovereignty ever since the Kingdom of Piedmont-Sardinia purchased it in 1729, but failed to register the transaction, thus invalidating the sale. Even though Seborga hasn't been recognized as an independent principality since this time, Carbone claimed that it retained its sovereignty. As the *Times* reports, "After convincing his Seborgan neighbors of their true significance, Giorgio Carbone was elected prince in 1963. He gracefully accepted the informal title of His Tremendousness, and was elected prince for life in 1995 by a vote of 304 to 4."[1]

I love his title: His Tremendousness!

And His Tremendousness went about setting up his country in a suitably tremendous fashion. The *Times* reports, "Prince Giorgio established a palace, wrote a Constitution, and set up a cabinet and a parliament. He chose a coat of arms, minted money (with his picture), issued stamps (with his picture) and license plates, selected a national anthem and mobilized a standing army, consisting of Lt. Antonello Lacala. He adopted a motto: *Sub umbra sede* (Sit in the shade)."[2]

The *Times* reporter who wrote the obituary obviously had fun talking about Giorgio Carbone and his royal tremendousness. It seems like Prince Giorgio had fun himself. He drove a black Mercedes with the official license plate of the Seborgan government number 00001. Although he received no salary, and as the *Times* reports, "it is not clear that he was offered one," he did regularly enjoy the ham and cheese from the village shop, which he considered a royal prerogative. And in a 1993 interview with *People Magazine*, Prince Giorgio said his dedication to Seborga was

1. Martin, "Giorgio Carbone," A47.
2. Ibid.

so complete that he remained unmarried, explaining that he "loved all his female subjects equally."[3]

Now, you may be wondering why I'm talking about Prince Giorgio of Seborga on Christmas. Well, for a couple of reasons. First, I really like the story. But second, and more importantly, it provides an interesting way into the story of the nativity in the Gospel of Luke. In Luke's telling of the birth of Christ, he draws a sharp contrast between the worldly power of Caesar Augustus, the most powerful person on the planet, and Jesus Christ, born a helpless child in the backwater town of Bethlehem. And the contrast between Caesar and Christ has a certain ironic character to it. We could say that all the trappings of the mighty Caesar Augustus are being lampooned in the way similar to the *Times'* story about Giorgio Carbone and His Tremendousness. In Luke's mind, all human pretensions to majesty and royal power, even when they are held by the true Caesars of the world, seem, from the perspective of the birth of Christ, like so many Prince Giorgios, starting their own countries, writing their own constitutions, and printing their own money with their pictures on it. Perhaps it is no surprise that Caesar Augustus actually did some of the same things as Prince Giorgio. We have coins from his reign minted with Caesar's image on one side and an inscription on the other calling him "savior" and "god." There is an ancient monument to Caesar's glory that bears an inscription calling him "the savior of the whole world."[4] Another stone inscription declares "the birthday of the god [Augustus] has marked the beginning of the good news for the world."[5] Caesar Augustus was also hailed as the bringer of peace, the *pax romana*. And remember, "Augustus" was a title. He was the August One, Augustus. You know, kind of like, His Tremendousness.

So when the story of the birth of Christ begins with a decree going out from the Emperor Augustus, we should see the irony. The one who thinks of himself as the most powerful man on the planet, whom many people viewed as savior and god, is actually, unwittingly carrying out God's plans for the birth of the true Savior of the world, who will be not the August One or the Tremendous One, but a helpless child. The birthday which is the beginning of the good news for the whole world is

---

3. Ibid.
4. Myra inscription, see Ehrenberg and Jones, no 72.
5. Priene inscription 40–42, see Dittenberger, *Orientis Graeci Inscriptiones* II, no 458.

not of the god Augustus, but of the baby Jesus. The peace of the world will not be brought at the sharp end of a sword, the *pax romana*, but through the ministry of the heaven-born Prince of Peace, the *pax christi*. We can almost see Luke smiling as he tells a story about the God who loves to turn things upside down, who, as Mary says in the Magnificat, "brings down the powerful from their thrones and lifts up the lowly." Think of the topsy-turvy nature of the angel's words to the shepherds tending their flocks by night: "For behold, I bring you good news of great joy which will be for all people; for to you is born this day in the city of David a Savior, who is Christ the Lord. And this will be a sign for you: you will find a babe wrapped in swaddling cloths and lying in a manger."

A babe wrapped in swaddling cloths and lying in a manger.

Not Caesar Augustus.

Not His Tremendousness.

But a baby, a helpless child lying in a manger.

Why would God choose to save the world through the birth of a baby rather than through one of the mighty Caesars of this world? Babies can't talk so they can't proclaim themselves to be gods and saviors. They can't print money with their pictures on it. They can't raise armies and conquer nations. They can't really do much of anything, except coo and cry and sleep. And smile when they see their mother's face and reach out and clasp their tiny hands around our fingers and fill our hearts with love.

Isaiah says, "For unto us a child is born. For unto us a Son is given. And his name shall be called, Wonderful Counselor, Mighty God, Everlasting Father, the Prince of Peace."

Now, do I truly understand this? Can I really wrap my mind around God coming to us in the form of a helpless child?

No, I cannot. It is a mystery. It is a wonder. And at Christmas time every year, I feel like a child again, and marvel at the wonder of it all. God with us. Emmanuel. A babe wrapped in swaddling cloths lying in a manger, and the angels singing glory to the new born king.

It is a mystery that I will never understand.

But I do think it is telling us something important about the way God is present to us and to this beautiful but hurting world of ours. Apparently, God chooses not to be present in this world through displays of great power and majesty. Pyrotechnics are the stuff of movies, not the gospels and not of Christmas. Rather, God chooses to be with us in our vulnerability and weakness. Caesar Augustus is not Lord and Savior. In a certain sense, in God's eyes, all human pretensions to royal power and divinity seem like so many Prince Giorgios proclaiming their own tremendousness. It is not in our power or in our accomplishments or in our tremendousness that God is found. Rather, God is found in our lowliness, our weakness, our vulnerability. As our hymn puts it, "Mild he lays his glory by."

Again, this is a mystery that I will never really understand, the mystery of God with us, Emmanuel. Why is it that God's presence is more fully known in humility and vulnerability than power and achievement? I don't know. I can't understand it.

But I have experienced it. And from many conversations, I know a lot of people who have experienced it too. The God who meets us in the midst of our struggles and sorrows. The God who meets us in tiny hands and sudden smiles. The God who meets us in small tasks and daily bread.

Why is it that we feel God's presence when we cut out the pretense and the puffing up? Why is it that God meets us in our humility rather than in our arrogance? Why is it that God is present not in our augustness or in our tremendousness, but in our honesty, humility, humanity?

I don't know, but that is where, time after time, people tell me they meet God in their lives. When we are honest, when we are vulnerable, when we admit our helplessness, when we cry out in pain or delight, God is present. It is in our common humanity, beautiful but broken, that our incarnate Lord keeps meeting us.

For unto us is born this day in the city of David a Savior, who is Christ the Lord. And this will be a sign for you: you will find a babe wrapped in swaddling cloths and lying in a manger.

And his Name shall be called, Wonderful, Counselor, Almighty God, Everlasting Father, the Prince of Peace.

A Christmas Prayer

Amy Richter

Part of the wonder of Christmas Eve is the possibility of the meeting of worlds, the coming together of time. We sing, "The hopes and fears of all the years are met in thee tonight." Though we live so long after those events in Bethlehem, tonight we find ourselves at the manger. In our mind's eye, we see the holy family in the stable, the mother tired, but radiant; the breath of the animals visible in the cold night air. We hear the lowing of the cattle and the rustle of straw. But most of all, we gaze in wonder at the baby, this long-expected child.

What would we say if we were there? What would we add to Mary's contented sighing and Joseph's protective, "There, there"?

As with all babies, just his existence is a gift. And as with all babies, it's not just his infancy, but his future we imagine and dream of and long for. But with this baby, this little one named Jesus, we have seen his future. We have glimpsed what lies ahead for him and what it means for us. So, what do we say to him as we take our place at the manger tonight?

In 1994 the Rev. Richard H. Schmidt wrote a reflection in *Episcopal Life* magazine entitled, "Christmas: Let Me Hold You, Dear Little Jesus."[6] Inspired by his image of holding the infant Christ, here are some words for our hearts' prayer on this Christmas Eve:

Little Jesus, let us hold you now. On this holy night, when you are a newborn baby, let us cradle you in our arms. Let us hold you and keep you warm. Now, while you are small and vulnerable, let us watch over you. We want to hold you now, because many times in time to come, you will hold us.

Rest well, sweet baby. Rest your tiny hands. For though you are the King of kings, you will touch no silk, you will carry no gold. You will grasp no earthly scepter, sign no imperial decrees. You will use your hands for far more precious works: touching a leper's wounds, wiping away a widow's tear, blessing and breaking bread, and giving it to your friends. Your hands, now so perfect, so tender, so tiny, will someday be wounded for us.

Sleep well, sweet baby. Rest your tiny eyes. For someday you will look at the world and you will see the pain and loneliness and ache that humans bear. You will look at us and see us just as we are, with all our sins and loveliness both. You will look and see the Christ within each one of us, and you will try to teach us to see it too.

Hush now, sweet baby. Rest your tiny mouth. For someday from your mouth eternity will speak. Your tongue will summon the dead to life. Your words will define grace, pronounce blessing, teach, and paint pictures with words so we too might see our eternal God the way you know God to be. Your mouth will speak forgiveness to those who wrong

---

6. Schmidt, "Christmas," 14–15.

you, will invite us to paradise to be with you forever, will send us forth in your name to all the world. Your words will echo down through centuries, bringing meaning and hope to our lives.

Rest now, tiny child. Rest your infant feet. For someday you will walk many miles to bring good news to the poor, to proclaim release to the captives. Someday you will stride out in power across billowing waves in a storm-tossed sea. Someday your feet will be anointed with oil by a woman who prepares you for death, and your feet will bear the same nail prints as your hands. Rest your feet now, for someday millions will follow in your footsteps.

And sweet little baby, with your little heart, how much love you will show. Rest now. And let us hold you on this holy night, for someday, you will hold us. Someday we will feel lost and lonely. Someday we will wonder—is this all there is? What does it mean? What am I here for?

Then you will come to us. You will not be a helpless infant then. You will come as our Wonderful Counselor, our deliverer, our Good Shepherd. You will search for us. You will call us each by name. And when you find us, you will rejoice. You will invite us to your banqueting table and nourish us with your very self. You will remind us that we belong to you; we are yours.

Little baby, let us hold you on this holy night, for someday you will hold us. Someday we will feel deep sadness and sorrow. Something will happen in our lifetimes that grieves us so deeply that we may wonder where you are. But you will come to us, then, not as a helpless baby, but as the Prince of Peace. You will remind us of the promises of God, of the strength of hope, of God's deep loving kindness, God's steadfast love. You will hold us close, and if we are quiet enough to hear, you will whisper to us that all will be well. All manner of things shall be well. You will tell us that you are here for us always, not just when we are empty enough to know we need you. You walk beside us, offering us your peace every day.

Sweet infant redeemer, let us hold you on this holy night, for someday you will hold us. Someday we will grow old or sick, our bodies will fail, and it will be time for us to rest from this world. Then you will come to us, not as a vulnerable baby, but as Mighty God, Everlasting Father. You will welcome us into eternal light and life. You will welcome us to a heavenly feast prepared since the beginning of time, a home and a place for us.

A Man, A Woman, A Word of Love

You will do all of these things for us at great cost to yourself. You will teach us the meaning of giving, all that we have and are, on behalf of goodness and love, no matter the cost.

But that will be someday. Tonight we adore you as a baby. We welcome you as a helpless, vulnerable babe, as the Almighty God who became a child so we could become full mature human beings; who was wrapped in swaddling cloths so we could be unraveled from the snares of death; who came on earth so we could live beneath the stars; who had no place in the inn, so you could prepare for us mansions in heaven; who became poor, so we could become rich; in whose weakness is our strength. This is the night, the wondrous night when we creatures hold our creator. This is the night of grace, when the Lord of heaven and earth stoops down, reverses roles, and allows us—the finite—to serve the infinite God.

And so, little Jesus, on this one night, let us hold you.

And let us whisper now the thanks that will be yours for all the years to come. Thank you, Jesus. Thank you for loving us. We love you too.

3

Manifest Love—Sermons for Epiphany

FIRST SUNDAY AFTER THE EPIPHANY: THE BAPTISM OF OUR LORD, YEAR B

Mark 1:4–11

John the baptizer appeared in the wilderness, proclaiming a baptism of repentance for the forgiveness of sins. And people from the whole Judean countryside and all the people of Jerusalem were going out to him, and were baptized by him in the river Jordan, confessing their sins. Now John was clothed with camel's hair, with a leather belt around his waist, and he ate locusts and wild honey. He proclaimed, "The one who is more powerful than I is coming after me; I am not worthy to stoop down and untie the thong of his sandals. I have baptized you with water; but he will baptize you with the Holy Spirit." In those days Jesus came from Nazareth of Galilee and was baptized by John in the Jordan. And just as he was coming up out of the water, he saw the heavens torn apart and the Spirit descending like a dove on him. And a voice came from heaven, "You are my Son, the Beloved; with you I am well pleased." (NRSV)

A Man, A Woman, A Word of Love

Know Thyself

Joseph S. Pagano

If you lived in the ancient world, and if you were about to make a major decision or embark on a major undertaking, and if you had the means, you would probably try to consult the Oracle at the Temple of Apollo at Delphi. And as you were entering the Temple, if you looked up, you would see inscribed on the lintel, the famous Greek phrase *gnōthi seauton*, "Know Thyself." This phrase was so important that it was attributed to several great philosophers including Thales, Socrates, and Pythagoras. The Latin poet Juvenal took it one step further and claimed the phrase descended from heaven itself. The phrase has even made it into American popular culture in the film, "The Matrix," where a Latin version, *temet nosce*, appears inscribed over the entrance to the Oracle's kitchen. From the Temple of Apollo at Delphi to the Oracle's kitchen in "The Matrix," the phrase "Know Thyself" has been understood as the beginning of wisdom.

The exhortation to know ourselves has also been central to the religious quest. The Psalmist queried, "What is man that thou art mindful of him?" St. Augustine and John Calvin affirm that true knowledge of ourselves leads to knowledge of God, and true knowledge of God leads to knowledge of ourselves. The quest for truth, goodness, and beauty, and the quest for God, often begins with the question of our own identity, with the admonition to know ourselves.

Who am I? What is my true identity? Where do I find my deepest self? These are perhaps the most important questions we will ever ask. And we ask them again and again throughout our lives: in childhood, in adolescence, in adulthood, and in old age. Often times after major events, such as marriage, the birth of a child, the death of a parent, or the loss of a job, we return to these questions: Who am I? What is my deepest and truest self? And the answers we come up with have probably changed many times during the course of our lives. Ever go back and read something you wrote in high school or college and wonder "Who was that person?" But we keep asking these questions because we know something important is at stake. We may think to ourselves: If I can just figure out who I truly am, what I am truly meant to be and do, then it seems like everything would finally fall into place, then my life would finally be whole and true and good.

The church is an appropriate place, perhaps the most appropriate place, to ask these questions, and to ask them with great honesty and with great care. Not because the church has all the answers. God knows it doesn't. Rather, we ask these questions in church because they matter. And because they matter, we ask these questions within that most intimate of experiences, within the context of prayer. With the utmost care and the utmost honesty, we ask the question of who we are as we stand starkly before the presence of God. With all our doubts, with all our fears, with all our finitude and all our failings, we open ourselves up to the divine and we ask: Who am I?

In the present day, with the frenetic pace of modern life, and with all the various demands on our time and attention, we often answer the question of who I am with a laundry list. We say things like, I'm from New Jersey, I'm a teacher, I'm married, I'm into sailing, I'm a gardener, I'm a Green Bay Packers' fan, I'm a jazz buff, I'm an avid golfer. In many ways, we are what H. Richard Niebuhr calls practical polytheists. The polytheist, according to Niebuhr, has many interests, but no center that can bring wholeness and order to their lives. Leaping from one interest to the next, they lack an enduring and integrated sense of self. James Fowler, in his book *Stages of Faith*, recalls a *New Yorker* cartoon that showed two female college students talking to each other. The subject was one women's latest boyfriend. She gushes to her friend and says, "He's into scuba diving, motorcycle scrambling, bluegrass banjo picking, pottery making, Haiku poetry, and Gupta Yoga! He's a real Renaissance Man!" Fowler remarks, "Whatever else he may be or become, I'll wager her boyfriend is a polytheist."[1]

We are all probably more polytheistic than we would like to think. We feel ourselves pulled in many different directions by many different interests. The result is that we live with a diffuse pattern of faith and identity. The various strands and threads of our identity are never drawn together into a whole cloth. Our identities feel fragmented and frayed.

One way out of this polytheistic predicament is to choose one thing among our many interests and raise it to utmost significance. Feeling ourselves frayed and spread thin, we take something like a job, a nation, a political party, even a church, and raise it up to become the ultimate source and center of all meaning and value in our lives.

---

1. Fowler, *Stages of Faith*, 19.

A Man, A Woman, A Word of Love

Are there any workaholics here today?

James Fowler tells a story of a top-flight surgeon, who defined himself by what he did. By chance, the surgeon ran into his minister in the hospital. The surgeon let himself go and talked of the pressures in his life, the professional burdens he carried, and the family strains he lived with. After a time his pastor put to him a question.

"Doctor," he said, "Who are you when you're not an M.D.?"

Stunned, but only for a moment, the surgeon replied, "By God, I'm always an M.D.!"

The pastor replied, "Yes, and that's just the problem."[2]

It is a problem when we define ourselves by what we do, because at some point we realize that we are more than our jobs. At some point, we realize our careers cannot provide us with the wholeness and meaning we long for, because at some time we will no longer be able to do what we are doing, and then we will be confronted with that same, deep question, "Who am I?"

In our Gospel lesson for today, we hear a different answer to this question. It is the story of Jesus' baptism. Mark tells us that after Jesus had been baptized, the heavens were opened, and the Holy Spirit descended upon him, and a voice came from heaven saying, "You are my beloved Son; with you I am well pleased." Notice, the voice does not say, "You are my beloved carpenter, with your woodworking I am well pleased." It does not say, "You are my beloved peasant revolutionary, with your ideology I am well pleased." No. The voice from heaven says, "You are my beloved Son, with you I am well pleased." Before Jesus does anything, before he embarks upon his public ministry of teaching and healing, prior to any definition of himself in terms of what his interests are and what he may say and do, Jesus is identified as the beloved child of God.

On this day, when we remember the baptism of our Lord, we also remember our own baptisms. And as we recall our own baptisms, when we were adopted as God's own children, we remember that the words spoken to Jesus are also spoken to each and every one of us. To you and to me and to all of God's children, God declares, "You are my beloved child, in whom I am well pleased." Not, "You are my beloved worker, in your sixty-hour work-week I am well pleased." Not, "You are my beloved republican, in your smaller government I am well pleased." Not, "You are

2. Ibid., 20.

my beloved democrat, in your liberalism I am well pleased." No. In the baptism of our Lord, we hear the great promise and the great truth that we are all the beloved children of God, first and now and always.

Who are we? The beloved sons and daughters of our loving God. And in this truth lies our deepest and truest identity. All the various strands of our lives—husband, wife, father, mother, nurse, social worker, music lover—come together in this truth. The deepest truth of our deepest selves is that we are all, each one of us, the beloved children of God.

In an interview with David Frost, Maya Angelou once talked about how the knowledge of God's love for us can change our lives. Angelou says, "Really. The idea that it, this creation, creator, it, loves me, me—not me generically, but me, Maya Angelou—is almost more—it is more than I can comprehend. It fills me. It enters and makes me go inflate like a balloon." She continues, "I can't know it too frequently. I can't know it completely. My heart might burst. My veins might boil up, and my blood might boil up in my veins. My eyes would pop out. My navel would thump. My feet would grow about six inches on either side. Really it has a physiological impact on me."[3] I suppose, we should allow Angelou a little poetic license. But she is trying to express the inexpressible. She is pointing us to the potentially life-changing impact that the truth of God's love for us can have when we really know it, when we really experience that love in the core of our being. As Angelou says in her memoirs, "God loves me. Each time I allow myself to say the words I am suffused with tears of gratitude and wonder. And I am reestablished as a giving, living, full human being with every right to everything right here on this earth."[4]

We are the beloved children of God. It is powerful stuff. If people really believed that, who knows what would happen. And yet, every time we gather together as a Christian community, that is essentially the message we proclaim. The theologian Ernesto Cardenal puts it this way, "Like a lover who thinks unceasingly of his distant beloved, so You, my God, have dreamed of me since long before I was born, dreamed of me from all eternity."[5] Archbishop Desmond Tutu says, "God loves us now and God will always love us, all of us good and bad, forever and ever. His love will not let us go, for God's love for us, all of us, good and bad, is unchanging,

---

3. Frost, "An Interview with Maya Angelou," lines 7–13.
4. As quoted in Brussat, *Spiritual Literacy*, 310.
5. Cardenal, *To Live is to Love*, 47.

is unchangeable." He continues, "there is nothing I can do to make God love me more, for God loves me perfectly already. And wonderfully, there is nothing I can do to make God love me less. God loves me as I am to help me become all that I have it in me to become, and when I realize the deep love God has for me, I will strive for love's sake to do what pleases my Lover."[6] The great cellist Pablo Casals once expressed this truth when he thought about what we should teach children. He said, "We should say to each of them: Do you know what you are? You are a marvel. You are unique. In all of the world there is no other child exactly like you. In the millions of years that have passed there has never been another child like you . . . You have the capacity for anything. Yes, you are a marvel."[7]

Imagine what it would be like if you really knew the truth that God loves you. Not just a general abstract truth about God's universal love, but the strong, particular voice that proclaims, "You are my beloved son, you are my beloved daughter, with you I am well pleased." It's almost more than we can comprehend. It might fill us up; inflate us like a balloon. Our hearts might burst. Our veins might boil up. Our eyes might pop out. It might feel like the heavens were torn apart or the Spirit like a dove descended upon us.

My brothers and sisters, do you know what you are? You are a marvel. You are unique. In all the years that have passed, there has never been another like you. God loves you for all eternity. Like a lover who spends all his time thinking of his distant love, God has been thinking of you since before you were born. There is nothing you can do to make God love you more and nothing you can do to make God love you less. Our adoption is forever. You are the beloved sons and beloved daughters of God, with whom he is well pleased.

Know thyself!

Nothing Between Us

Amy Richter

Perhaps you have experienced an epiphany of some sort during your life, a moment when you realize a truth, behold a reality, see something for

---

6. Tutu, *No Future Without Forgiveness*, 85.
7. Kahn, *Joys and Sorrows*, 295.

Manifest Love—Sermons for Epiphany

what it is for the first time truly. An epiphany experience touches you and shapes you, and, if you let it, may sustain you long after the moment has passed. Epiphany comes from the Greek word for appearance or manifestation. In this Epiphany season, we celebrate the manifestation of Jesus Christ in the world and tell stories of how Jesus made God known to the people around him. The Feast of Epiphany was during this past week, on January 6. On January 6, we remember the story of the Magi, the wise men, the first Gentiles to worship the baby Jesus, the first Gentiles to whom the identity of Christ was made manifest. Starting today, we tell stories about the adult Jesus and his ministry. And those stories begin with today's Gospel reading, the story of Jesus' baptism, a moment of epiphany.

I had a moment, if not of epiphany, then at least of greater understanding, one clear night on a little jetty of land in Nova Scotia. Joe and I were spending our summer holiday in a house in a remote area of this maritime province, a place with no light pollution, and at night, amazing starry skies. One night the stars were so many, so brilliant, so close, it looked like the sky was a big black bowl turned upside down, with holes punched in it with light blazing down from above. Or, the sky was a big dome and brilliant stars were somehow fixed to the inside of the glass.

I know better, of course. I know that the sky is not an upside down bowl, and in our scientific age I understand that I was just one small person looking up at the sky that extends up and out and out and out from one small planet that travels around the sun, one of billions of stars in a galaxy in a universe so huge it boggles the mind.

The sky is not a bowl, but when I saw the sky that night I could understand how ancient people could look up at the starry, starry sky and imagine the sky as a big dome with holes punched in it here and there to let light or rain or snow through. That's sort of how our forebears in faith, the ones whose stories became the Bible, saw it. "In the beginning," we read in Genesis 1:1, "God created the heavens and the earth." On the first day, God created light. On the second day, God created a firmament, something firm between the earth and what's above it. Listen to how this firmament is described: "And God said, Let there be a dome in the midst of the waters, and let it separate the waters from the waters. So God made the dome and separated the waters that were under the dome from the waters that were above the dome. And it was so. And God called the dome sky."[8] The ancient Hebrews understood the earth to be like a round plate surrounded by water on the sides, and above and beneath as well. A firm bowl, that firmament, kept the waters out, but had gates or windows in it to let the rain and the snow through. From below the plate, the waters came through as rivers and seas and could be reached by wells or bubble up in springs, but the earth stood firm on pillars sunk into the waters like the pilings of a pier.

In this view, the world looks rather like a wooden plate that you might put a wedge of cheese on, with a glass dome put over top of it. Below the plate, and all around that dome is water, and above that water some place is the dwelling place of God.

If you keep that picture in mind, some other Old Testament stories make more sense. Like in the story of Noah, where we hear, "In the six hundredth year of Noah's life, in the second month, on the seventeenth day of the month, on that day all the foundations of the great deep burst forth, and the windows of the heavens were opened."[9] Imagine: God reaches down to the dome of the sky, opens up some windows, and lets water pour through to flood the earth. This is how the ancient Hebrews pictured it.

It's a pre-scientific view of the earth, and my point in mentioning it isn't to say how far we've come in our understanding. The point is to better understand Mark's telling of the baptism of Jesus.

So hear the good news of Jesus Christ as recorded in Mark's gospel. "In those days,"—in *those* days when people still thought of the sky like a dome and God is up there looking down, and John the Baptist is preaching, "Repent and be baptized," and being pretty open about the fact that God could reach down through one of those heavenly windows and squash those who do not repent like a bug—"In those days, Jesus came from Nazareth in Galilee and was baptized by John in the Jordan. And just as he was coming up out of the water, he saw the sky ripped open and the Spirit descending like a dove on him. And a voice came from heaven, 'You are my Son, the Beloved; with you I am well pleased.'"

Mark says the sky was ripped open.

Just about a month ago, during the season of Advent, we heard a reading from the prophet Isaiah, "Oh that you would rend the heavens

---

8. Genesis 1:6–8.
9. Genesis 7:11.

and come down!"[10] Isaiah wants God to tear open the sky, smash through that dome. And I get the feeling he thinks God should come down here and kick some people in the pants to set things right. "Tear open the heavens and come down!" Today we hear Epiphany's answer to Advent.

The sky is ripped open, says Mark, and here comes, not a deluge of water to wipe us all out, not an angry God to take some names and knock some heads together, but the Holy Spirit, fluttering down like a dove, and the voice of God saying, "Here is my Son, the Beloved." In this single, startling act, God our Creator smashes through the barrier that has separated us. No longer can we imagine the Creator on one side of the firmament and creatures on the other. God demolishes the barrier not in anger, but in love, and in that moment, God bridges the gap between us forever, starting from God's side.

I believe God never intended for us to be separated from God like we imagined, to watch us from above like someone looks down on a slice of cheese under a glass. God didn't separate from us, but we separated ourselves from God, and if anyone put up a firmament between us, maybe it's a barrier of our own making. It may be that our early ancestors, as maybe some of us do today, just felt safer thinking of God on the other side of the glass up there and away. But our Bible tells us that God doesn't want to be separate from us. In the story of the Incarnation, the sending of Jesus Christ to be a human for us, we meet Jesus living with us, under the same sky we do. In this Epiphany story we hear of God trying to become known to us by cracking through that dome and calling out, "Here is my Son! If you want to know me, get to know him." And at last, the sky is ripped open, the dome is cracked, the barrier is gone.

This image of a ripped-open sky shows us God's determination to know us, and to be known by us. Epiphany is illustrated in this action, but that's not the end of it. Epiphany happens over and over again as God comes to us again and again, breaking down all those barriers we put in God's way. We see this in the story of Jesus as he heals and teaches, feeds and prays, and dies, all so we can be close to God.

There will also be another tearing apart, a ripping open, in Jesus' story. When he is crucified, the curtain in the temple that separates the holy of holies from the rest of the temple will be torn in two, so that the holiest place is open to everyone, just as the crucifixion makes possible salvation for all.

10. Isaiah 64:1.

At Jesus' baptism, the sky is torn open, the barrier comes down. At our own baptisms, the same happens. In our baptism we are also named as God's own children. In your baptism, you received the pledge that in you God is well-pleased. Because of Jesus Christ, there is nothing that can separate you from God's love. You can allow the fruits of faith grow in you and let them show forth in your life. You may find that God so fills you with love, that you have love to give away, love that can spill over into acts of love for others.

In baptism the sky is ripped open, the barrier is gone. This is a promise guaranteed by God who tears the heavens open, who tears temple curtains open, who cracks our hearts of stone, to come to us, to hold us close and whisper to us, "You are my beloved child. I am with you always, and I will never let you go."

FOURTH SUNDAY AFTER EPIPHANY, YEAR A

Micah 6:1, 6–8

Hear what the LORD says: Rise, plead your case before the mountains, and let the hills hear your voice. Hear, you mountains, the controversy of the LORD, and you enduring foundations of the earth; for the LORD has a controversy with his people, and he will contend with Israel. "O my people, what have I done to you? In what have I wearied you? Answer me! For I brought you up from the land of Egypt, and redeemed you from the house of slavery; and I sent before you Moses, Aaron, and Miriam. O my people, remember now what King Balak of Moab devised, what Balaam son of Beor answered him, and what happened from Shittim to Gilgal, that you may know the saving acts of the LORD." "With what shall I come before the LORD, and bow myself before God on high? Shall I come before him with burnt offerings, with calves a year old? Will the LORD be pleased with thousands of rams, with ten thousands of rivers of oil? Shall I give my firstborn for my transgression, the fruit of my body for the sin of my soul?"

He has told you, O mortal, what is good; and what does the LORD require of you but to do justice, and to love kindness, and to walk humbly with your God? (NRSV)

Matthew 5:1–12

When Jesus saw the crowds, he went up the mountain; and after he sat down, his disciples came to him. Then he began to speak, and taught them, saying:

> *"Blessed are the poor in spirit, for theirs is the kingdom of heaven.*
> *"Blessed are those who mourn, for they will be comforted.*
> *"Blessed are the meek, for they will inherit the earth.*
> *"Blessed are those who hunger and thirst for righteousness,*
>   *for they will be filled.*
> *"Blessed are the merciful, for they will receive mercy.*
> *"Blessed are the pure in heart, for they will see God.*
> *"Blessed are the peacemakers, for they will be called children of God.*
> *"Blessed are those who are persecuted for righteousness' sake,*
>   *for theirs is the kingdom of heaven.*
> *"Blessed are you when people revile you and persecute you and utter all kinds of evil against you falsely on my account. Rejoice and be glad, for your reward is great in heaven, for in the same way they persecuted the prophets who were before you."* (NRSV)

A Good Cry

Joseph S. Pagano

Have you ever heard the phrase "a good cry"? On occasion I have heard people say things like, "I just want to go home and pull the covers over my head and have myself a good cry." Maybe you have experienced a "good cry" yourself. It sounds like a paradox, and yet, many people report that they actually feel better after crying. One study found that 85 percent of women and 73 percent of men say they feel better after crying. As counterintuitive as it may sound, it seems like sometimes crying can be good for you.[11]

Writers and poets have long known this truth. Shakespeare wrote, "To weep is to make less the depth of grief."[12] Alfred Austin wrote, "Tears are the summer showers of the soul."[13] Shakespeare and Austin are pointing to the truth that weeping actually lessens our grief and sorrow. What is really interesting is that some scientists can now explain why this is so.

Tears are actually quite amazing. Researchers speak of three different types of tears. The first are called basal tears that are made up of mucus and water and salts. Every time we blink, we spread these tears over our eyeballs keeping them well lubricated. They also contain antibodies and enzymes that defend the eye from microbes and bacteria. The amazing, unnoticed production of basal tears keeps our eyes well lubricated and healthy. The second type of tears we produce are irritant or reflex tears. They are made of the same elements as basal tears and also work to protect us. When some unwelcome intruder hits the eyeball, like a piece of dust or sand, these tears flow. They serve to flush the eyeball and cleanse it from irritants. Physiologically, basal and reflex tears keep the eyeball happy and healthy.

The third type of tears, emotional tears, are the ones we normally think of when people cry. It is here that the research gets interesting. It turns out that emotional tears are quite different from the other types. Emotional tears contain a lot more proteins than the others. William Frey, director of the Dry Eye and Tear Research Center in St. Paul, Minnesota, has found that the proteins in emotional tears are hormones that build up in the body when it is under stress. These substances prepare the body to cope with stress. However, after the stressful event is over, their continued presence would keep the body in a state of needless tension and arousal. Frey suggests that the purpose of emotional tears is to reduce the excessive amounts of proteins that accumulated after a stressful event. Crying emotional tears, in a certain sense, flushes these proteins from the body, and sure enough researchers have found that crying lowers the

---

11. Foreman, "Why Cry?" G8.
12. *Henry VI*, Part III (2.1.85).
13. Austin, *Savonarola*, 264.

blood pressure, pulse rate, and body temperature, and results in more synchronized brain-waves. As these things are generally considered to be measures of tension, the conclusion from these studies is that crying is good for you.

So I guess we can really say that there is such a thing as a good cry. However, our Gospel lesson for today pushes us to ask a further question: Is there such a thing as a blessed or holy cry? In the Sermon on the Mount, Jesus says, "Blessed are those who mourn, for they will be comforted." This beatitude seems to be saying that beyond sometimes having a good cry, there is something that we may call blessed weeping or holy tears. What might this be?

The first thing we might ask about Jesus' statement "Blessed are those who mourn" is what are they mournful about? If we take into consideration the context of the Sermon on the Mount, then I don't think Jesus is really talking about hurt feelings here. Rather, in the Sermon on the Mount, Jesus is describing what life in the kingdom of heaven is like. He says things like "blessed are the poor in spirit for theirs is the kingdom of heaven," "blessed are the meek, for they will inherit the earth," and "blessed are the merciful for they will receive mercy." These are the values that are considered blessed in God's desires for the world. However, it quickly becomes apparent that these sayings of Jesus are actually turning the world's value-system upside down. In the beatitudes, Jesus is saying that it is the poor in spirit, the meek and the merciful who are truly blessed in God's kingdom, but we live in a world where the self-sufficient and the power-brokers are thought to be blessed. So when Jesus says, "blessed are those who mourn," he is not talking about mere sadness or crying, but rather lamenting over all the hurt and pain in the world. It's the mourning that grows out of hearing the message of God's kingdom, God's desires for peace and mercy, and the awareness of the difference between the world as it is and the world as God desires it to be. God's people grieve over the spoiling of God's purposes for the world and the deep pains of human society. The world is out of joint and people raise their lament, "O God, there is so much hurt and pain in the world; do not let your world hurt this way forever." It is this type of mourning that Jesus seems to be to be talking about when he says, "Blessed are those who mourn."

So there does seem to be a type of mourning that is also blessed, a type of tears that are also holy. In the midst of the tears, in the midst of the mourning, there is also blessing. And yet, while the blessedness is experienced in the present, it is not based on the present, but rather on hope for the future, in the assurance of God's coming kingdom, in the promise that someday they will be comforted. As paradoxical as it may sound, there is blessedness in mourning right now when God's people live in the hope of the kingdom of heaven, where those who hunger and thirst after righteousness will be filled, where the merciful will receive mercy, and where the pure in heart will see God. Blessed are those who mourn right now, because they will be comforted. It does seem as though there is blessed weeping or holy tears.

In a recent book, Kimberley Patton and John Hawley talk about the power of holy tears. They begin by reflecting on a passage from the Talmud that says, "But though the gates of prayer are closed, the gates of weeping are not closed."[14] They write, "Isn't weeping a kind of prayer, a liquid entreaty? Yet it is not prayer, not utterance. Inchoate, messy, 'running,' a sign of being 'overwhelmed' or helpless, even unable to speak ('choked up'), how could tears in this Talmudic passage from a tradition that so enshrines the oral and written holy word, supersede *prayer*? How could weeping, born in the matrix of inarticulate despair beat out praying ... as a better portal to heaven?"[15] Yet, as they point out, in many religious traditions "tears carry not only power but unique power: God is unable to ignore them, and the psalmist is compelled to remind Him of this: *Hear my prayer, O Lord, and give ear to my cry; keep not silence at my tears.*"[16] It seems as though tears have a power to attract God's attention that can be even greater than prayer.

Perhaps this is part of what Jesus means when he says, "Blessed are those who mourn, for they will be comforted." There are several passages in the Old Testament that suggest that tears are a powerful means of summoning God's attention. Psalm 51 says, "A broken and contrite heart, O Lord, You will not despise" (Psalm 51:17). Psalm 6 says, "I am weary with my moaning: every night I flood my bed with tears; I drench my coach with weeping, My eyes waste away because of grief; they grow weak because of all my foes. Depart from me all you workers of evil, for the Lord has heard the sound of my weeping. The Lord has heard my supplication; the Lord accepts my prayer" (Psalm 6:6–8). And in 2 Kings, when King

14. Babylonian Talmud, Tractate Berakhot 32b as quoted in Patton and Hawley, *Holy Tears*, 1.

15. Patton and Hawley, *Holy Tears*, 1.

16. Ibid.

Manifest Love—Sermons for Epiphany

Hezekiah is sick, he not only prays to God, but, we are told, he also "wept bitterly" (2 Kings 20:3). In response, the word of the Lord comes to Isaiah and says, "I have heard your prayer, I have seen your tears; indeed, I will heal you" (2 Kings 20:5). There seems to be a power in tears that evokes a response from God. When we cry to God, there is the expectation, the hope that God will hear our weeping, draw near to us, and heal us. *Blessed are those who mourn, for they will be comforted.*

Patton and Hawley also point out that in the Jewish tradition the God of Israel is said to weep himself in response to human weeping. The Jewish tradition does not see God as distant and cold and untouchable. Rather, it speaks of the pathos of God, of a God who is passionately connected and concerned with his people, of a God who weeps when his people weep. In his chapter on weeping in Jewish sources, Herbert W. Basser states that in Jeremiah God weeps and wails for God's people.[17] In Jeremiah 9:1, we hear, "O that my head were a spring of water, and my eyes a fountain of tears, so that I might weep day and night for the slain of my people." It is unclear whether the speaker of these words is the prophet or God. And yet, no matter who we take the speaker to be, it is clear that God is anguished and grieves for God's people. The Talmud takes up the theme of God weeping in Jeremiah. Reflecting on the passage from Jeremiah 13:17, "my soul will weep in secret for your pride; my eyes will weep bitterly and run down with tears," the Talmud pictures God retreating to his inner chambers to weep because he knows that the sound of his weeping would overwhelm the world. In a Hasidic reflection on this theme of divine weeping we hear that the *hasid* can join God in his inner chambers. As Rabbi Nehemia Polen says, the Hasidic teacher, Rabbi Shapiro, "embraces the midrashic image of God weeping alone in His Inner Chambers, and avers that the *hasid* can push in, join his tears with God's, communing with God in suffering, just as at happier times we commune with God in a shared joy."[18] What we see in these traditions is another dimension of holy tears, what Patton and Hawley call a mystical "communion-in-suffering" with the God of Israel. They say, "When the God of Israel weeps, as He does in response to human catastrophe in texts ranging from the rabbinic to the Hasidic, a certain ultimacy is implied. In divine weeping, God joins human beings in a mystical 'communion-in-suffering'

17. Basser, "A Love for All Seasons," 182.
18. Polen, "'Sealing the Book with Tears,'" 89.

that explodes questions of theodicy and instead both ratifies and transcends mortal grief."[19] So holy tears, blessed mourning, somehow unite us to God in a mystical communion-in-suffering, where God's grief both recognizes and validates our human grief and also overcomes that grief.

The Episcopal priest Betsee Parker spoke of hearing God weeping while she was blessing the remains of the victims of September 11 terrorist attacks in New York. Her account bears a striking resemblance to the Talmudic tradition of God weeping in His Inner Chamber. She was working in the morgue at Bellevue Hospital when she says she heard, "a very deep, very frightening deep moaning sound," that she interpreted as God weeping.[20] Parker said it was like walking in on someone who was weeping in private, like she "saw someone sitting and weeping quietly and you had not meant to see this."[21] She says, "To hear this—and it was inescapable; wherever I walked in that place that day, it pierced me deeply. *The feeling was terrifying—of what in the world was I doing hearing this sound of the weeping of the depths of the—of God?*"[22] Asked if she wanted to leave, Parker says, "Desperately. It made me want to run and hide. I felt so inappropriate. I didn't know—I felt like I was—you know—walking in on God."[23]

Parker was asked why she thought God was weeping. She replied, "Well, my sense was that [it was because] those whom he loved the dearest had been ravaged and hated and destroyed by those whom he loved the dearest."[24]

Is there such a thing as a good cry?

Is there such a thing as blessed mourning?

Are there holy tears?

In our Gospel lesson for today, Jesus said to the crowds and the disciples who came to him, "Blessed are those who mourn, for they will be comforted."

---

19. Patton and Hawley, 2.
20. Reverend Betsee Parker, "'Send Thou Me,'" 287.
21. Ibid., 288.
22. Ibid.
23. Ibid.
24. Ibid., 287.

Manifest Love—Sermons for Epiphany

Where the Beatitudes Make Sense

Amy E. Richter

It happened again recently at a Walgreen's. It was supposed to be one of those *I'll just run in quickly and pick up that one little thing and be right out* trips. But it turned into one of those check-out experiences that seems to happen to me often: whichever line I get into suddenly grinds to a halt.

The line wasn't long—six people held a few items each in their red plastic baskets—but it was brought to a standstill by a woman with a very bad cold who couldn't find her money. Her nose was red, her lips were chapped, and she had that faraway look of someone who hasn't slept well. She held a rumpled white Kleenex to her nose with one hand, while with the other she rifled through a large brown vinyl purse that she had propped open on the counter. Others waiting behind her in line were getting fidgety—okay, irritated, more accurately—as she rummaged in her bag and then emptied the contents of her coat pockets onto the counter: more wrinkled and wadded-up tissues, a ring of keys, a hair clip, grocery store coupons, gum wrappers, cough drops, but no wallet, no money. As she continued her search and those behind her sighed or turned to texting on their cellphones for solace, the cashier stood patiently and encouraged the woman. He smiled at her. He told her not to panic. He asked if she wanted him to hold her things while she checked in her car. He was perfectly calm in the midst of the growing anxiety around him.

Eventually the woman found her money—it was in a pocket on the inside of her coat—and paid for her purchase. As she picked up the plastic sack holding her items and headed for the door, the cashier called out with a smile, "Have a blessed day!"

He repeated this greeting to each of the customers as we made our way to the counter, showing the same calmness and cheerfulness to each person, "Have a blessed day!" And each person seemed a little more relaxed after having their own moment with the cashier. A young man looked up from his cell-phone and said, "uh, thanks." A woman in a suit un-hunched her shoulders, and smiled back.

As I paid for my purchase, I noticed the cashier had a white button with green lettering pinned to his shirt just below his employee nametag and that more of these buttons were for sale, hanging on a red ribbon behind him. The message on the button explained his peaceful demeanor: "Too blessed to be stressed."

A Man, A Woman, A Word of Love

In today's reading from the Gospel according to Matthew, from the beginning of what's called Jesus' Sermon on the Mount, Jesus pronounces a series of blessings. This must be one of the most beloved passages in the New Testament. But we hear it so often we may miss the shock of it. Jesus says, "Blessed are the poor in spirit . . . Blessed are those who mourn . . . Blessed are the meek . . . Blessed are you when people revile you and persecute you and utter all kinds of evil against you falsely on my account . . ."

Mourning? Hungering and thirsting for righteousness? Trying to make peace? Being persecuted? This sounds like a recipe for stressing, not blessing! Have a blessed day? If these are the blessings on offer, we may want to get into a different check out line.

The blessings Jesus describes are certainly different from what we may normally perceive as blessings. People in the situations Jesus describes do not fit with the aspirations of much of our culture: being self-sufficient, not being poor in spirit; being entertained and happy, not mourning; being outwardly powerful, not meek; being safe and admired, not persecuted and reviled. Some translators use a different word than "blessed" to heighten the upside-down-ness of Jesus' words: "Happy" are those who mourn, or "honored" are the merciful, or "fortunate" are the peacemakers. Anyway you say it, though, Jesus' picture of blessings is not the usual picture of how the world works. The beatitudes have a beautiful ring to them, but do they really make any sense?

The Rev. Dr. Stephen Holmgren led a teaching weekend at St. Paul's Church in Milwaukee when Joe and I served there. Canon Holmgren wrote the book in the Episcopal Church's New Teaching Series on ethics, a book called *Ethics After Easter*.

Canon Holmgren presented two different pictures of how we orient ourselves to God and other aspects of our lives, two different views of how the world works. In both, there is someone in the middle of a circle, and around the edges of the circle are the various interests and concerns and people in our lives.

In one picture of the world, the someone in the middle of the circle is Me. And around me are things like family, friends, work, concerns, hobbies, and God. In this Me-centered view of the world, I try to address the various things that are out there around me. I try to figure out how much time and energy I should give to the various things out there in my orbit. In terms of ethical thinking, I ask, What can I do? What am I permitted?

Notice that God is in my orbit too. I think about God. I try to put God in the right place, give God God's due. I try to bring the sacred into my daily life. And in my Me-centered view of the world, I may think that God is so pleased to be part of my picture, to have made it into my circle, that God responds by being my friend and helping me.

Where this picture is caught up short is by today's first lesson, where the prophet Micah says, "Walk humbly with your God." Not, take your God for a walk. No—walk humbly with God.

And so a second picture is a God-centered picture, where God is in the center, and I am in the circle around God, along with friends and family and concerns and work and hobbies. God alone fills the center. In this picture, I don't bring the sacred into daily life, I realize that we are always on sacred ground. In this picture, we are led to ask, not, what can I do? but, how does God want me to live? To what kind of life am I called?

This is the world in which the beatitudes make sense, a world in which God is the center, where the world existed before I was here to notice it, where God's values undergird and determine reality. I am part of a constellation of beings around God. I am called into relationship with God and others, not so that I can be served and accumulate things and feel fulfilled only when my perceived needs are met, or rely on the false notion that I can be independent and self-sufficient. God calls me into relationship with God and others and invites me into full and abundant life in which we are blessed when we hunger and thirst for righteousness, when we work for peace, when we acknowledge sorrow and authentically mourn, when we show mercy, when we are reviled and scoffed at, even persecuted because we are followers of Jesus Christ who try to live out God's vision in Micah where we do justice and love kindness and walk humbly with God.

Can we embrace Jesus' description of blessings, seeing them as a way to life? As we ask questions like, How does God want me to live? To what kind of life am I called? can we risk accepting these blessings as part of the answer?

Each of us finds ourselves in different situations, different relationships, with different opportunities, confronting different challenges. And yet, we are given some common principles by which to live. The beatitudes have a lot to do with our Baptismal Covenant, the promises we make, or are made on our behalf, at our baptism. Our baptismal identity has to do not only with what we believe, but how we are to live.

How are we to live?

Jesus says, "Blessed are the poor in Spirit."

We are blessed when we come before God, not full of our own accomplishments, not burdened with possessions, not searching for earthly security; but standing before God open-handed and open-hearted, ready to receive God, knowing we are utterly dependent on God.

Jesus says, "Blessed are the merciful, for they will receive mercy."

Our reconciliation with Christ, our being forgiven, means that we are to show mercy, even as we have received mercy.

Jesus says, "Blessed are the peacemakers, for they will be called children of God."

In a world torn apart by violence, in our homes, in our cities, in our nations, we are to be agents of reconciliation, peace, and healing.

Jesus says, "Blessed are you when people revile you and persecute you and utter all kinds of evil against you falsely on my account."

It's risky business, proclaiming the Good News of God in Christ. It can be uncomfortable. It can make others uncomfortable. Proclamation is risky, but rewarding, even blessed.

Soon we enter the season of Lent, traditionally a time set aside in the church to prepare for the renewing of our Baptismal vows, or maybe even to be baptized if you are not already, at the Easter Vigil. Lent is a time for intentionally exploring our lives in light of the love of God as we experience it in Christ Jesus, a time for asking, How does God want me to live? To what kind of life am I called? Will I live in this world, seeing it as a Me-centered world, or a God-centered world, the only world in which the beatitudes make sense, a world in which they can bring comfort, joy, and challenge? During these days before Lent, I invite you to think about how you may use these coming forty days of preparation for saying your own "Yes" to God once again.

Our life as citizens of God's kingdom begins at the baptismal font. This life of living as baptized children of God, sons and daughters called to a rich life, a blessed life, is a life of surprising reversals, where mourning brings blessing, showing mercy brings honor, working for peace brings happiness, where being reviled for the sake of Christ brings even joy.

Have a blessed day.

FOURTH SUNDAY AFTER EPIPHANY, YEAR B

Mark 1:21–28

They went to Capernaum; and when the sabbath came, he entered the synagogue and taught. They were astounded at his teaching, for he taught them as one having authority, and not as the scribes. Just then there was in their synagogue a man with an unclean spirit, and he cried out, "What have you to do with us, Jesus of Nazareth? Have you come to destroy us? I know who you are, the Holy One of God." But Jesus rebuked him, saying, "Be silent, and come out of him!" And the unclean spirit, throwing him into convulsions and crying with a loud voice, came out of him. They were all amazed, and they kept on asking one another, "What is this? A new teaching—with authority! He commands even the unclean spirits, and they obey him." At once his fame began to spread throughout the surrounding region of Galilee.

Classroom Management

Joseph Pagano

If knowledge is power, then teachers are powerful people. Teachers have the power to change lives, for good or for ill. Teachers can create, with their words and their gestures, new worlds of possibility and meaning. They have, within their hands, an awesome power to inspire and to heal people's lives, or the power to terribly hurt and harm young lives. Most of us probably have stories about some caring or inspiring teacher to whom we feel forever indebted for helping us to grow and to learn. Many of us also have stories about the damage done to us by a cruel or uncaring teacher. Teachers are powerful people.

As someone who spends a lot of his time in the classroom, I think a lot about what makes for good teaching. Good teachers are obviously people who know their subject matter. But we all know that this isn't enough. There are plenty of brilliant people who aren't very good teachers because they can't communicate very well with their students. So good teaching requires more than knowledge. It also requires an ability to engage students, to understand their thoughts and concerns, to get close to students. We've all, I hope, had some good teachers, folks who were caring, concerned, and engaged, who taught us a great deal.

There are also, I think, some teachers who are not only good, but great. Great teachers are not only people from whom we may have learned a great deal, but those few teachers who have changed our lives. In contrast to good teachers who, because of their concern for students, draw close to them, empathize with them, great teachers always keep some distance between themselves and students because of their loyalty to a larger truth. Great teachers are slightly off-putting, because students, like all humans, are usually looking for the easiest way to the truth, and would much prefer to stick with their assumptions than to engage in the often painful process of rethinking and change. Great teachers keep their distance so students will have the space in which transformation can take place. They are so committed to the subject they serve that they are willing to forego us liking them so that we may have the space to examine our lives in light of the demands of truth. Great teachers don't just teach us things. Great teachers create a space in which our lives may be changed by confronting us with the demanding truths they serve above all else and which they mediate to us in their teaching.

So teachers are powerful people. While good teachers engage students and get close to them, great teachers remember to put some distance between themselves and students. They do this in order to create the space in which students can change. And we know that change can be scary and that change can be painful. So we try to avoid change, even when we know deep down that we need to, even when we know that we need to let go of the ideas and habits and fears that are diminishing our lives. But great teachers don't let us get away with it. Great teachers challenge and confront us with the truth that they serve beyond all else. And it is in light of the truth—sometimes scary, always demanding—that genuine transformation can take place. The truth may set us free, but nobody said it would always be easy. Great teachers, loyal to the truth beyond all else, are powerful people who can powerfully transform our lives.

This morning I want to focus on Jesus as teacher. I do this not only because I think teaching is an important topic, but also because that is what our Gospel lesson for today wants us to focus on. Mark writes, "they were astounded at his teaching, for he taught them as one having authority, and not as the scribes." Now a whole lot of things are going on in this passage, many of them strange and wonderful. But today I want to focus on how Jesus wasn't just any old teacher, a teacher like the scribes, but rather how he was a great teacher, someone who taught with the power to transform lives.

In this wonderful and in many ways challenging story, I think we have a picture of Jesus as a great teacher. You see, contrary to many sweet and saccharine portraits of Jesus, he was not a warm and cuddly figure. He wasn't like one of those merely good teachers who are caring and engaged and empathetic in our modern sense of the words. You know the type—button down shirts, cardigan sweater, wire-rim glasses, loafers. Rather, he was a great teacher, someone utterly devoted to the truth he proclaimed. He was also probably a little frightening. He came on the scene proclaiming, "The Kingdom of God has drawn near. Repent and believe in the Good News." He was on fire with the message that the Kingdom of God had drawn near, and he was utterly devoted to the service of this truth. So when Jesus taught, he exposed people to the power and brightness of God's presence, and in the power of that presence, in the power of that message, people's preconceptions and prejudices were laid bare and fell away. People felt themselves exposed and stripped of their defenses in the presence of the truth. In the teaching of Jesus, not just a good teacher, but a great teacher, people felt called to change, to renewal, to genuine transformation. As Mark says, "The people were astounded at his teaching because he taught them as one having great authority."

In our Gospel lesson, we immediately get an example of the great power and authority of Jesus' teaching. As a classroom teacher, I must admit, I love this part. While Jesus is teaching, an unruly young man starts screaming at the top of his lungs, "What do you have to do with us Jesus of Nazareth? Have you come to destroy us?" Now as folks in the education business might say, Jesus has got himself "a classroom management problem." They might also go on and try to psychologize the problem by saying that a student who interrupts his teacher and starts screaming at him probably has a problem with authority figures. But, to tell the truth, I've never much liked the term "classroom management" and the psychologizing that usually goes along with it. At official faculty workshops, we might discuss things like this by asking, "Now, how might Dr. Pagano have responded to the adversarial relationship his student was setting up between himself and the teacher?" "How might a teacher diffuse such a situation?" But at the lunch table or in the faculty lounge, when we were just talking, we would revert to implicit theories of demon possession. We would say things about our bad students like, "What has gotten into that young man today?" or "What crawled up inside of him and died?" At official faculty meetings we would talk dispassionately about all the latest theories in human development and all the latest classroom management techniques. But when some student started screaming his precious little head off in the middle of a long semester, we didn't want a theory and we didn't want a technique. We wanted an exorcist. I have seen full professors, authors of many books, extremely enlightened men and women, reduced to shaking their heads and saying things like "God, help that child!" If you have spent any significant time in the classroom, I bet at some point in your career you spoke like someone who still believes in exorcism or at least wishes it were an option.

So when Jesus was teaching in the synagogue and the man with the unclean spirit starts screaming, notice that Jesus does not calmly explain to him why his behavior is inappropriate and he does not go on to explain the consequences that will follow if he continues with his inappropriate behavior. No, Mark tells us, "Jesus rebuked him saying, 'Be silent, and come out of him.'" To put it in more modern terms Jesus said, "Shut up and get out!" Now, my friends, that is what I call "classroom management." And Mark says, "the unclean spirit . . . came out of him." Those were the days! No trying to understand where the student is coming from. No saying things like, "Gee, Johnny, it sounds like you are really upset about something." No invitation to meet and talk about this after class. Just "Shut up and get out." Like I said, that is what I call classroom management!

But, then again, Jesus was a great teacher, a powerful teacher, someone who could transform lives with his powerful message. And all the students, all the other people in the synagogue exclaimed, "What is this? A new teaching—with authority!"

Some time ago, Don Browning wrote a book called *The Moral Context of Pastoral Care*. This was a book for ministers on how to help people with their problems. Browning claims that in today's world when we talk about human problems we end up reducing things to the psychological. All human pain becomes a problem of psychological maladjustment, or chemical imbalance, or of infantile experiences. Yet, Browning says, there are many problems that are more cognitive than psychological. That is, there are many problems that are more about not knowing well than about not feeling well. Many people are in pain because they are confused. Modern life has so perplexed them, things seem so chaotic and confused, that many people are miserable. There is so much that seems out of kilter, chaotic, and frightening in our world, that modern life seems as chaotic and confused as that poor, demented young man screaming his head off in the synagogue.

One of the reasons, I think, why we are here this morning is because we are searching for answers to life's big questions, searching for reasons why things happen the way they do, searching for some sense in the midst of the confusions of modern life. We have been bombarded with facts and figures. We have been overloaded with information. What we need is not more information, but rather to somehow see the larger picture, to see a larger pattern to help us navigate the tricky terrain of modern life. What we need is a teacher, a great teacher. We are looking for a teacher with genuine power and authority. We are looking for a teacher who can help us change, who can help us find genuine transformation and meaning. We are looking for a teacher who can restore us to wholeness and sanity. We are looking for a teacher who can calm our raging spirits, who can still our battered souls, who can fill us with the peace that passes understanding. We are looking for someone who teaches us to love our God, to love our neighbors, to forgive our enemies, and who blesses us even when we are poor in spirit. We are looking for a great teacher.

Lord Jesus Christ, our Great Teacher, speak words that calm our troubled souls and fill us with your peace. Amen.

What Happened at Church Today?

Amy Richter

I think it's fair to say that we don't expect surprising things to happen in church every Sunday. We may be open to something new or different, we may even want something new or different, but we don't necessarily expect something different, and we certainly don't expect to be surprised by the preacher. I truly hope that people who worship in our parish on Sundays think they usually hear good sermons and that a bad sermon or a dud of a sermon would come as a surprise.

But surprising things do happen in worship, right? Things we hadn't planned for crop up, like the bulletin blooper that elicits a laugh where we aren't expecting it. We once printed a prayer, I'm embarrassed to admit, that praised Jesus for bringing the gift of correctly spelled, but theologically heretical "immorality" rather than "immortality" to the world. Things we hadn't anticipated happen, like the toddler who breaks free from the pew where her parents think they have her hemmed in, and runs up the aisle toward the altar sprinkling cheerios from a Ziploc baggy as she goes, while shouting, "Hooray! Hooray!" Things we couldn't expect fly in, like birds through the open front door on a warm day, or swoop down from the rafters like bats, and then, you know you can talk all you want, but that sermon is pretty much over—especially when your competition is from bats. Put an "Amen" on it and move on.

But sometimes the surprises in worship aren't just amusing or distracting. They are genuinely good, sometimes even transformative, like worship was that day in the synagogue when Jesus showed up.

Whatever the reason worshippers were there that Sabbath, we have no reason to expect that they were expecting to be surprised when they went to worship that morning. Maybe they were just happy to have made it into their usual pew with all the children's shirts on frontwards and the crumbs from the granola bars eaten in the mini-van on the way wiped off. Maybe some of them were wondering why, other than a habit that made them feel a little more peaceful, they were even bothering this week. Truth be told, when the scribes teach, there isn't much to it, nothing much really to address the confusion, the deep concern, the pain they actually struggle with in real life. Maybe some of them were looking vaguely forward to the comfort of the liturgy, with its predictable shape, its words you can say without even really having to think about it much, an oasis of calm in the midst of weeks filled with too much activity, too much unpredictability. They sit back, settle in for the sermon.

And then Jesus comes in.

Jesus comes in as the guest preacher for the day and begins to teach them, and—surprise!—there is something about Jesus' teaching that makes them take notice. It isn't his reputation—very few of them had ever heard of him. It isn't his credentials—his bio in the bulletin doesn't list any degrees or even seminary training. The crowd of disciples he came in with who have taken all the seats closest to the refreshments table looks like a bunch of ordinary guys and smells faintly of fish.

Manifest Love—Sermons for Epiphany

But there is something in his very presence and words that makes them think something new is going on here. Here, in this man Jesus, is something worth paying attention to. Suddenly folks are sitting a little straighter in their seats. A man stops clipping his fingernails. A woman stops making her grocery list. A member of the choir puts down the Sabbath crossword puzzle and nudges the soprano sitting next to her. Even a nine-year-old, working on the search-a-word in the children's bulletin, puts his colored pencil down for a moment and looks up at Jesus. Suddenly, everyone is paying attention, eagerly hanging on to Jesus' words, wondering what he's going to say next.

But just as suddenly, from a pew in the corner a shriek goes up, and it's not a toddler whose brother has yanked his favorite blanket away. The voice is too low, too throaty, a cross between a growl and a scream, as if several mouths are vocalizing at once. This Sabbath service is just full of surprises.

The shrieking comes from a man who cries out, "What have you to do with us, Jesus of Nazareth? Have you come to destroy us? I know who you are, the Holy One of God!" The man is obviously deeply disturbed. It's the ushers' worst nightmare, and people are horrified this is happening during such a good sermon.

But before the head usher has a chance to mobilize his team and get this guy out to the narthex, Jesus shouts back, "Be quiet!"

Everyone may be surprised he said it out loud—guest preachers are usually more polite—but they are relieved he did it. But Jesus has another surprise in store, something no one expects. Jesus says, "Come out of him!" The man shakes violently, shrieks one last time, and collapses as if all the fight has gone out of him. The wild look in his eyes is gone; the color has returned to his cheeks; a look of calm relief suffuses his face.

Coffee hour that Sabbath is a little different as well. There's lots to talk about, and it all focuses on one thing: "What is this? A new teaching—with authority!" This Jesus has authority, even over powers of evil.

It's kind of interesting, isn't it, that what they say after Jesus sets the man free from the unclean spirit is not, "What is this? A new exorcism—with results!" Or, "What is this? A new healing—with noise reduction." No, what they say is "A new teaching—with authority."

We don't actually know what Jesus had been preaching before he was interrupted. We aren't given his text or any lines from his sermon. But somehow, when he heals the man, when he sets him free from what was tormenting him, the people who have seen Jesus' action, link it with his words.

He doesn't just proclaim good news, he makes good news. He doesn't just announce the nearness of the Kingdom of God—they watch as he rescues a man captive to the powers of evil and hand delivers him over the threshold of the Kingdom. That's what gets their attention on that Sabbath day in Capernaum. He has the power to transform lives and set people free. He has authority.

Authority is not just power. It's not the same as brute force, or making people do what you want. Here's a definition of authority that Wayne Meeks uses: "The [person with authority] is a person who augments power by inspiring and focusing the power of others."[25] The one with authority expands power and enhances power by inspiring and focusing the power of others.

Jesus sets the man with the demon free, not to show off or disrupt the liturgy, but to give the man his own ability back. Jesus teaches, not to show us how smart he is, but to give us wisdom to use, life-giving, peace-making, joy-enhancing words for us to live by. Jesus calls us, not to add to his list of accomplishments by attracting many followers, but in order to send us out, to use our gifts and opportunities and abilities and, yes, power to do God's work in the world. "You will do even greater things than these," Jesus tells his disciples in the Gospel of John. His authority, his power, expands power by inspiring and focusing the power of those who follow him.

I wonder what happened the next Sunday in that synagogue, after Jesus had left town and taken his preaching on the road. Did the people come expecting a little more from their worship experience? Did the regular resident preachers spend a little more time on their sermon preparation? Did people invite some of their friends who hadn't come to worship in awhile—"something different is going on in worship these days"?

Or, were people a little relieved when, by next Sabbath, Jesus had moved on to another town, had another preaching engagement in another place? Did the ushers go over their emergency plans a little more carefully, try to figure out how to prevent that kind of outbreak from happening again in the future? Check the demoniacs at the door. Keep the guest preacher away from the unpredictable.

25. The definition comes from John Howard Schütz and appears in Meeks, "Social Functions of Apocalyptic Language," 702.

But Jesus would not be kept away from the unpredictable, from the broken, the painful, the uncomfortable. Jesus will not be kept away from the chaotic, the uncertain, the suffering, and anxious. The Jesus who embraces all our sorrows and all our joys, all our struggles and all our hopes, all our fears and all our longings is still present, still in our midst, still showing up for worship when we do, still offering us the presence of the living God here, now.

Richard Foster has said of worship, "It is not for the timid or comfortable. It involves an opening of ourselves to the adventurous life of the Spirit."[26] Isaac Pennington writes that when people are gathered for genuine worship, "They are like a heap of fresh and burning coals warming one another as a great strength and freshness and vigor of life flows into all."[27] Wonderful images, I think. And I've been fortunate to experience that kind of vigor and warmth in worship sometimes.

It was two weeks into my freshman year in college. I hadn't cried when my parents dropped me off on my first day, although my mother did. I was off on a new adventure for which I had been prepared, about which I was excited. I was excited to meet my roommate in person, transform our dorm room into our new home, find out if we had similar tastes in music, decide whether to leave our dorm single beds as bunks or set them both on the floor. To taste freedom from direct parental influence and rules was exciting, even if that freedom was contained by a structured environment that included a dining hall where someone still cooked all your meals and classes where professors took attendance. The chance to learn new things, read new books, be exposed to new ideas, engage with new people, learn from new teachers, was something I was looking forward to. No time for homesickness.

That lasted exactly ten days. Our posters were hung in our dorm room, we had gone with the bunks, our first papers were due, and I was severely homesick. I missed my friends. I missed my parents, my brothers, my own room, and the cat who curled up on my feet each night. I missed people who already got me and understood my jokes. I was tired of introducing myself and trying to learn new names. I was tired of trying to figure out if I would fit in, how I would fit in, with whom I wanted to fit in. I was only three hours by car from home, but I felt a continent away.

---

26. Foster, *Celebration of Discipline*, 173.
27. Quoted in Foster, 172.

My longing for home settled like a weight on me. I had chosen this school, in part, because it felt like a good fit for me. Was I wrong? My desire to go home was edged out only slightly by my desire not to feel like a complete failure.

It was the third week in September. Our school held a Wednesday night communion service in the choir loft of the chapel. We sat on the choir risers and the pastor, one of the theology professors, wore his street clothes and a green stole. Three students played guitars and led the singing. The pastor talked about grace and home and God loving all of us. He said that Jesus was close to us and wouldn't leave us alone. I don't remember the text of his sermon, but as it has become embedded in my memory, it's Romans 8, where Paul proclaims that nothing—not death or life, nor angels, nor rulers, nor professors, nor syllabi, nor assignments, nor all the miles between you and home, nor anything else in all creation—will be able to separate us from the love of God in Christ Jesus our Lord. Something about the personal nature of God's care stuck like a burr onto my sleeve during a walk in a sunlit meadow. The notion of the wideness of God's mercy snuck up during that sermon, embedded itself in me, and left a lump in my throat that was still there when we came to communion.

The pastor said the words of institution and held up a round loaf of bread. He broke it in two at the words of the fraction, then tore the bread into smaller pieces. He put a piece of this consecrated loaf into my hand and said, "the body of Christ given for you." And I heard the *you* as *me*. I held it in my palm, could see the fibers that entwined to compose it, could smell its fragrance. The piece weighed so little, but it was a fragment of a larger whole.

I thought of all the years that I had been receiving communion, the Sunday mornings when bread had been placed into my open and outstretched hands—"held like a throne to receive a king"—the thin wafers that came in wax paper-covered rolls that the ladies of the altar guild unwrapped and set out before the service, the special leaven-free bread my mother had made for Maundy Thursdays, the pieces of pita that were used. I thought of the hands that had placed the bread there—usually my father's, but also my grandfather's and other pastors, and youth leaders, and retreat leaders. I thought of the words they had used when placing the bread—words that were not their words, not their property, and not said because they knew *me* or loved *me*—although some of them no doubt did—but because they knew and loved God, and they knew God loved me and wanted me to have *this* bread, blessed and broken and shared by God's Son for *me*. And it didn't matter if the bread came from a kitchen three hours by car from where my family still lived, or whether my mom had baked it, or some altar supply company; this bread really came from God, from the same loaf that people had been taking and blessing and breaking and sharing in the name of Jesus since that first night in an upper room while disciples who were strangers in that place gathered in a city far from home because they felt like they were supposed to be there that night. And Jesus pressed a piece of the broken bread into their hands and said, "this is my body for you" and maybe they heard the you as *me* or maybe they were still too surprised to hear that body was bread and bread was body, but there on that night in the choir loft, I heard that Jesus had given this bread for me and I was connected with him and with all those altar guild ladies and pastors and everyone I had kneeled next to at communion or ever would.

The students started to play "Abide with Me" on their guitars and voices intertwined and people sang in harmony and it sounded so good we sang it through again: *I need thy presence every passing hour; what but thy grace can foil the tempter's power? Who, like thyself, my guide and stay can be? Through cloud and sunshine, Lord, abide with me.*[28] And then a moment of silence before the pastor gave the benediction, "The Lord make his face to shine upon you and be gracious to you, lift up his countenance upon you and give you peace." And God did.

We filed out of the loft and out through the big glass double doors of the chapel. The night was clear and the sky was ablaze with stars that seemed very close to the earth. Some students started to hum the hymn as we walked, hand-in-hand, back toward the dorm.

---

28. Abide with Me. Words: Henry Francis Lyte (1793–1847). Music: *Eventide*, William Henry Monk (1823–1889).

4

Redeeming Love—Sermons for Lent

FIRST SUNDAY IN LENT, YEAR A

Genesis 2:15–17; 3:1–7

The Lord God took the man and put him in the garden of Eden to till it and keep it. And the Lord God commanded the man, "You may freely eat of every tree of the garden; but of the tree of the knowledge of good and evil you shall not eat, for in the day that you eat of it you shall die." Now the serpent was more crafty than any other wild animal that the Lord God had made. He said to the woman, "Did God say, 'You shall not eat from any tree in the garden'?" The woman said to the serpent, "We may eat of the fruit of the trees in the garden; but God said, 'You shall not eat of the fruit of the tree that is in the middle of the garden, nor shall you touch it, or you shall die.'" But the serpent said to the woman, "You will not die; for God knows that when you eat of it your eyes will be opened, and you will be like God, knowing good and evil." So when the woman saw that the tree was good for food, and that it was a delight to the eyes, and that the tree was to be desired to make one wise, she took of its fruit and ate; and she also gave some to her husband, who was with her, and he ate. Then the eyes of both were opened, and they knew that they were naked; and they sewed fig leaves together and made loincloths for themselves. (NRSV)

Matthew 4:1–11

Then Jesus was led up by the Spirit into the wilderness to be tempted by the devil. He fasted for forty days and forty nights, and afterwards he was famished. The tempter came and said to him, "If you are the Son of God, command these stones to become loaves of bread." But he answered, "It is written,

> *'One does not live by bread alone,*
> *but by every word that comes from the mouth of God.'"*

Then the devil took him to the holy city and placed him on the pinnacle of the temple, saying to him, "If you are the Son of God, throw yourself down; for it is written,

> *'He will command his angels concerning you,'*
> *and 'On their hands they will bear you up,*
> *so that you will not dash your foot against a stone.'"*

Jesus said to him, "Again it is written, 'Do not put the Lord your God to the test.'"

Again, the devil took him to a very high mountain and showed him all the kingdoms of the world and their splendor; and he said to him, "All these I will give you, if you will fall down and worship me." Jesus said to him, "Away with you, Satan! for it is written,

> *'Worship the Lord your God,*
> *and serve only him.'"*

Then the devil left him, and suddenly angels came and waited on him. (NRSV)

A Man, A Woman, A Word of Love

To Whom Do You Beautifully Belong?

Joseph S. Pagano

To whom do you beautifully belong?

This question comes from a play by Henry James called "The High Bid." It's from a scene where a gentleman, Captain Yule, is talking to a butler, Chivers, in the country house Yule has just inherited from his great uncle. At one point in the conversation Yule asks, "What are *you*, my dear man?" a question trying to get at the butler's identity. At first the butler doesn't catch the drift, so the man asks again, "I mean, to whom do you beautifully *belong*?"[1] In this passage, I think Henry James is suggesting that the question of identity is tied to the question of belonging: What are you? To whom do you beautifully belong?

I love that question.

Now, with Henry James, we need to be aware of his irony. James was fond of having his characters call each other "beautiful" and "marvelous," when in actuality they were becoming more and more ugly in their behavior. What might to outward appearances seem beautiful was, in a moral sense, quite ugly. A less subtle example of this irony is found the language of my native state of New Jersey. When I would royally mess up and do something really stupid, my friends would say things like "That was just beautiful, Joe. Truly brilliant!" Now, it should be pretty clear that they didn't really think I was acting beautifully and brilliantly. Quite the opposite. Not exactly Henry James, but you get the point.

James's idea that the things that we belong to, the things we give our allegiance to, can subtly shape our characters, for good or for ill, is put to good use in Alan Hollinghurst's novel, *The Line of Beauty*. It's about a young man, Nick Guest, who gets caught up in the seemingly beautiful and grand world of some upper-middle class Brits in the 1980s, who turn ought to be quite ugly in a moral sense. Nick comes from more humble circumstances and he is attracted to a college friend's family because of their money, power, and success. But behind the grand parties and fabulous holidays, we soon see an underlying hypocrisy and ruthlessness that eventually turns on Nick himself. Nick desperately wants to belong to this powerful and attractive set, but what happens is that in the process

---

1. James, "The High Bid," 567.

of being welcomed into the family he himself becomes hypocritical and ruthless and quite ugly.

To whom do you beautifully belong?

Is this an ironic question?

Are the people or things or values that you put your trust in and pledge your loyalty to making you truly beautiful or actually quite the opposite?

How are our characters being shaped for good or for ill by the people and values and things we end up worshipping?

I raise these questions because this morning we have two classic biblical passages about worship and temptation. In our Old Testament lesson, Adam and Eve are tempted by the serpent to eat the forbidden fruit, and in our Gospel lesson Jesus is led into the wilderness where he is tempted by the devil. Now, there is an enormous amount of literature on the meaning and nature of the temptations in the garden and in the wilderness. You have probably heard hundreds of sermons on these passages, all of which have probably uncovered some important things. But this morning, I want to focus on just one aspect of these stories. I want to explore the questions of identity and belonging that they raise. In a certain sense, of both temptation stories, of Adam and Eve in the garden, and of Jesus in the wilderness, we could ask the question: to whom do you beautifully belong? And with Adam and Eve we see one type of response and with Jesus we see another.

With Adam and Eve, we all know the story. God created Adam and Eve, put them in the Garden to till it and care for it. They can eat of every tree of the garden, except for the tree of the knowledge of good and evil. Along comes the serpent and he starts asking some crafty questions: "Did God really say you shall not eat from any tree in the garden?" "Well, no, not from any tree, only the one in the middle of the garden, if we eat of that one, or even so much as touch it we will die." And so on and so forth, until they finally eat the fruit.

But what's the temptation really about? Is it really about eating a piece of forbidden fruit? Or is it about something else? There are lots of answers to these questions, but notice what the serpent says, "God knows that when you eat of it your eyes will be open and *you will be like God, knowing good and evil.*" Did you catch it? Did you hear the real temptation? "You will be like God." That does sound pretty good. Adam and Eve are creatures. They belong to God. As creatures they are given everything they need: a good world to live in and to work in. And yet, the serpent in his crafty way raises the question: "to whom do you belong?" *Well, God I suppose.* "But if you eat from the tree, then you will be like God. You won't belong to God anymore. You will be the sovereign lords of your own lives, knowing good and evil, belonging to no one but your own selves." Sounds pretty good. *Freedom. Power. Knowledge.* It's tempting, right? To be our own gods. To be lords of the world. To be like God. And they eat . . .

But do they become like God?

No. They become ashamed. They become aware of their nakedness. They fall from grace. When they belonged to God and lived as good creatures of their good Creator, everything was good. Indeed, it was very good. When they sought to "beautifully" belong to their own selves, rather than become like God, they fell into shame, they distorted the image of God in themselves, and what they knew was not good and evil, but rather their own shame.

As my friends in New Jersey might say, "That was really brilliant, guys. Just beautiful!"

To whom do you beautifully belong?

Is whom or what you are giving your ultimate loyalty to, your ultimate allegiance to, enabling you to become truly beautiful and good, or is it causing you to become quite ugly in a moral sense?

In the story of Adam and Eve we see creatures denying their dependence on God, their status as creatures, and ending up enslaved to their selves and their selfish desires. But in the story of the temptation of Jesus, we see a different response. Again there has been an enormous amount written on the three temptations Jesus' faces in the wilderness. But, again I want to focus on just one aspect of them. It seems to me all of temptations are about Jesus' identity, about whom he really belongs to. Notice how the first two temptations are phrased: "If you are the Son of God, command these stones to become loaves of bread." "If you are the Son of God, throw yourself down from the temple." Satan is tempting Jesus by questioning his identity as the Son of God. *If you are the Son of God.* The real kicker comes in the last temptation, "Bow down and worship me and I will give you all the kingdoms of the world and their splendor." Each temptation is, in its own way, about who Jesus is, to whom he belongs, and how he will or will not remain faithful to that identity. And unlike Adam and Eve, Jesus remains true to who he really is. He will not turn stones to bread, not because bread is a bad thing, but because we don't live by bread alone but by every word that comes from the mouth of God. He will not jump off the temple into the arms of angels because he will not put God to the test. And he will not bow down and worship Satan because he knows we are to worship God and serve him alone.

So for Jesus all the temptations are about his identity.

What are you, my dear man?

The Son of God.

And, then, as the Son of God, to whom do you beautifully belong?

The Lord our God and to him alone. Not to material power. Not to political power. Not to worldly success. Rather, to God and God's purposes and God's kingdom.

So in the story of Adam and Eve and in the story of Jesus in the wilderness we get contrasting responses to the problem of worship and temptation, to the question of to whom do we belong. Adam and Eve deny their identity as creatures of God and fall into shame. Jesus remains true to his identity as the Son of God and angels wait on him. Both stories raise the old question of whom or what we are going to worship? Whom or what is it that we really trust? Whom or what is it that we truly believe in? To whom or to what do we truly belong? Is it God or something less than God? And the answers to these questions are going to tell us a lot about our character, beautiful and good, or otherwise. As N. T. Wright puts it "You become like what you worship. When you gaze in awe, admiration, and wonder at something or someone, you begin to take on the character of the object of your worship. Those who worship money become, eventually, human calculating machines. Those who worship sex become obsessed with their own attractiveness or prowess. Those who worship power become more and more ruthless."[2] In the stories of temptation we hear basic questions about our identity and about whom we belong to. Will we belong to money or power or success? As beautiful and as attractive as things like this may seem, if we end up belonging to them we may become very ugly indeed. To whom do you beautifully belong?

Adam and Eve gave into the temptation, but Jesus did not. And because he did not, that is good news for all of us. He did not give into the temptation to be a mere earthly ruler who wielded only earthly power. Rather he remained true to who he was as the Son of God and to whom he truly belonged. And he stayed true to a ministry which did involve

---

2. Wright, *Simply Christian*, 148.

becoming the Lord of all the kingdoms of the world, but not by falling down and worshipping a false god, but by being nailed upon the cross. As disciples of Jesus Christ we face a similar temptation whenever we try to find some easier or more popular path to follow than the way of the cross. Whenever the creed of salvation through success gets substituted for the way of sacrificial love and costly grace, Satan smiles. Whenever we give our ultimate allegiance to that which is not God—to social standing or economic power or religious pretense—hoping that this will satisfy our deepest desires, then we succumb to temptation. The good news of the story of Jesus is that he did not succumb to temptation, he did not deny his true identity, he did not bypass the costly way of the cross. And in doing this, he shows us the One who alone deserves our complete and total worship, and the way we must travel if we are to become truly beautiful.

Who or what is it that we worship?

Or as Henry James might put it: "To whom do you beautifully belong?"

A Little Big Word

Amy Richter

Something my husband thinks about every year, just around the time Lent gets underway and it's still chilly and wintry where we live, is his desire to head down to Florida to watch professional baseball players in Spring Training. Joe would love to go watch his favorite players or the players who look promising this year participate in this annual ritual of getting ready for the official season.

I also have fantasies about heading somewhere sunny and warm this time of year, but in my version, there are no calisthenics, no warm-ups, no running of bases, or players doing drills. The lifting in my version isn't weights on a weight bench, it's paperback novels on a beach blanket. The adjustments in my version aren't to swings and stances, they're to the angle of the umbrella and the tilt of my lounge chair.

Still, I think Joe's version has more to commend it for Lent. Baseball players need to get ready for the season. They need the commitment of a period of time to prepare, train, practice, stretch, work out, recommit to discipline. I don't know if players enjoy Spring Training or not. I don't know if they would rather go straight into the regular season and skip all the stuff they have to do first to get ready. But there's no requirement that this time of preparation be gloomy or boring. People like Joe flock to see the practice and get excited about what may be possible for their favorite team and players because of what they see going on in Spring Training. Maybe Joe will actually get to go some year, and not just dream about it.

Lent is a time for exercising the muscles of our faith, of going into a training season of sorts to tend to the parts of our faith and discipline that have gotten weak or flabby, or to recommit to some healthy spiritual habits so our faith may grow and flourish, so we may actually live the life Jesus came to give us—an abundant life of joy and fulfillment no matter what comes.

Whether you like the thought of Lent as spring training or not, this morning we're going to engage in a little spiritual exercise that leads to abundant life. It is a hard exercise for many of us, even though it involves just a few actual physical muscles. But exercising these muscles, really, is part of Jesus' path to joy. Try it with me. Place the tip of your tongue behind your upper front teeth. Now as you start to push air through your vocal chords, bring your lips into the shape of an "o." Try it again. "N-n-n-o-o." It's a fairly simple exercise. You can do it sitting down or standing up. You can do it pretty much anywhere. But it can be so hard for so many of us to do. Our faces come equipped with everything we need, and yet, it really is a challenge. Who among us has not thought at some time, "I really should have said no"? Or, "why is so hard for me to say no"? "I'm going to have to learn to say no." Ever said it? Well, Lent is a fine time to practice.

Now if you are a parent, you may have actually no problem using this little word a lot. You may be thinking, practice? I am a pro. I heard a reporter on television say the average American toddler hears the word no as many as 400 times a day.[3] That's a lot of No! But other than through repetition with a two year-old, how's it going for you? Is it a little harder to say it for yourself?

Our Gospel story hinges on this tiny little word. Jesus says it, and everything is different because he does.

It should come as no surprise that right near the beginning of Luke's account of the good news of Jesus, there is this temptation scene. It may remind us that our whole Bible begins with a temptation story right near the beginning of it, right at Genesis chapter 3, if you want to look it up

---

3. Aria, "How to Say No," line 2.

A Man, A Woman, A Word of Love

sometime. The story about Adam and Eve, usually called the Temptation or the Fall, wasn't always interpreted in the way we've come to hear it, as the explanation for how sin came into the world. It wasn't simply a flat story that can lead us to sigh and say, "if only there hadn't been an apple," "if only Eve could have resisted," "if only Adam hadn't been away at the time—hey, where was Adam, anyway?"

Originally the story functioned as etiology, a multi-layered story to explain how we got here, why things are the way they are. This story pointed to human conundrums like, why is it that being told there's one thing you can't have makes you want it more than anything else in the world? Why do people betray and blame the people closest to them when things go wrong? Why are snakes so weird and creepy? Why is it really, really hard to say no?

It wasn't until the early centuries of the Christian church that the Church Fathers bundled all of these human predicaments together, seeing this story as the introduction of sin into the world and calling it the "Temptation and Fall."

And truth be told, it's not a bad summary to see many of our human problems coming from all the ways we think, "I can say yes," "I can go along with this," "I can handle it," when so many indications are to the contrary; saying, "sure, why not," when we've been explicitly warned, when we know better. When saying no takes fewer facial muscles but is so much harder to do.

The Adam and Eve story takes human freedom seriously and human limits seriously and says if we have a hard time saying no, we come by it honestly. It runs in the family.

But our family tree has some other important members as well. In today's Gospel lesson, Jesus faces temptations to say yes to using his gifts for his own benefit alone, to seek his own comfort, prestige, and power at the expense of his calling and purpose, to reject his baptismal identity as beloved child of God, to sever himself from his connection to God and God's purposes for him. For Jesus to say yes to Satan would be to pretend he hadn't just been forever connected to God and God's purposes. And Jesus says no.

If we take seriously that Jesus was completely human, even as he was completely divine, that he really was tempted in every way as we are, yet did not sin, then he said no, not by tapping into some superhuman strength, not by sending in his divine nature to do battle against all the devil's temptations. We know that's not the case because this was the very temptation Jesus was saying no to—he wouldn't call down special favors as the Son of God. If he would face the tempter and triumph, it would be as our brother, drawing only on the same kind of power you and I have as sons and daughters, God's dearly beloved children in baptism.

I wonder if part of the difference between our legendary first ancestors and Jesus was that Jesus trusted the power of community, and when push came to shove, Adam and Eve chose to go it alone. The snake said, "You don't need God. Did God really say you can't eat of this tree? What has God done for you lately?" Eve says, "Maybe you're right, I can handle this. I don't need God or God's advice, let alone God's pretty much straightforward commandment." Adam doesn't appear to have thought much at all. And when things really start to fall apart, it was every creature for him- or herself. Adam pointed at Eve, Eve at the snake, the snake just lay there sticking his tongue out . . . don't look at me. Instead of embracing, they pointed fingers. Instead of paradise, they got separation.

Maybe Jesus had not just the strength, but the courage to say no because he knew he wasn't in this alone. We think of the temptation of Jesus as a lonely time—he's out in the desert after all—who is out there with him? But Jesus goes out there led by the Holy Spirit. He goes out there, still damp from the Jordan water of his baptism, his ears still ringing with God's message to him: "you are my son, my child, my beloved." He goes out there with the spiritual company of his cousin John who baptized him, with the spiritual company of every other person who had waded through those baptismal waters before him. Jesus may have been out in the desert, but he was most decidedly not alone. Maybe the courage to say no comes from community. Maybe the courage to say no comes from a community that gives us the space to practice saying no. No to things we know will hurt us or others. No to things that will demean us or others. No to things we know are wrong or harmful or unjust. No to things that call us to be other than who we are: beloved children of God, worthy of dignity, bearers of no less than the image of God, each of us with our own purpose from God for the world.

It seems to me that denying ourselves, even giving up something for Lent, has gone a little bit out of style lately. People scoff, and maybe justifiably so, at the idea of giving up chocolate for Lent (have you tried it?), as if that's really going to make a difference. Many look down on the idea of giving up alcohol or fasting from television or email or whatever it is that has become routine. After all, if it's not really a problem for us, why deny ourselves?

But I wonder if to practice saying no now, in training for when things actually are a problem for us, may just be a good enough reason.

Practicing saying no to something that takes up more time or energy or money or appetite than it has to may be a good idea for helping us say no to things that really do compete for God's attention, whether God is calling to us outright, or through our neighbor, through our parish, through our child, our spouse or partner, through some inner voice that is trying to get our attention to call us to be more respectful of ourselves. To practice saying no now, so that we can say yes to some other more worthy things.

Lent reminds us that we have a choice to say no every day. Lent reminds us that we are part of a community that can help us discern and own and practice saying no. So we can say yes, to an abundant life in Christ, a life of resurrection joy.

FOURTH SUNDAY IN LENT, YEAR A

John 9:1–41

As [Jesus] walked along, he saw a man blind from birth. His disciples asked him, "Rabbi, who sinned, this man or his parents, that he was born blind?" Jesus answered, "Neither this man nor his parents sinned; he was born blind so that God's works might be revealed in him. We must work the works of him who sent me while it is day; night is coming when no one can work. As long as I am in the world, I am the light of the world." When he had said this, he spat on the ground and made mud with the saliva and spread the mud on the man's eyes, saying to him, "Go, wash in the pool of Siloam" (which means Sent). Then he went and washed and came back able to see. The neighbors and those who had seen him before as a beggar began to ask, "Is this not the man who used to sit and beg?" Some were saying, "It is he." Others were saying, "No, but it is someone like him." He kept saying, *"I am the man."* But they kept asking him, *"Then how were your eyes opened?"* He answered, *"The man called Jesus made mud, spread it on my eyes, and said to me, 'Go to Siloam and wash.' Then I went and washed and received my sight."* They said to him, *"Where is he?"* He said, *"I do not know."*

They brought to the Pharisees the man who had formerly been blind. Now it was a sabbath day when Jesus made the mud and opened his eyes. Then the Pharisees also began to ask him how he had received his sight. He said to them, "He put mud on my eyes. Then I washed, and now I see." Some of the Pharisees said, "This man is not from God, for he does not observe the Sabbath." But others said, "How can a man who is a sinner perform such signs?" And they were divided. So they said again to the blind man, "What do you say about him? It was your eyes he opened." He said, "He is a prophet."

The Jews did not believe that he had been blind and had received his sight until they called the parents of the man who had received his sight and asked them, "Is this your son, who you say was born blind? How then does he now see?" His parents answered, "We know that this is our son, and that he was born blind; but we do not know how it is that now he sees, nor do we know who opened his eyes. Ask him; he is of age. He will speak for himself." His parents said this because they were afraid of the Jews; for the Jews had already agreed that anyone who confessed Jesus to be the Messiah would be put out of the synagogue. Therefore his parents said, "He is of age; ask him."

So for the second time they called the man who had been blind, and they said to him, "Give glory to God! We know that this man is a sinner." He answered, "I do not know whether he is a sinner. One thing I do know, that though I was blind, now I see." They said to him, "What did he do to you? How did he open your eyes?" He answered them, "I have told you already, and you would not listen. Why do you want to hear it again? Do you also want to become his disciples?" Then they reviled him, saying, "You are his disciple, but we are disciples of Moses. We know that God has spoken to Moses, but as for this man, we do not know where he comes from." The man answered, "Here is an astonishing thing! You do not know where he comes from, and yet he opened my eyes. We know that God does not listen to sinners, but he does listen to one who worships him and obeys his will. Never since the world began has it been heard that anyone opened the eyes of a person born blind. If this man were not from God, he could do nothing." They answered him, "You were born entirely in sins, and are you trying to teach us?" And they drove him out.

Jesus heard that they had driven him out, and when he found him, he said, "Do you believe in the Son of Man?" He answered, "And who is he, sir? Tell me, so that I may believe in him." Jesus said to him, "You have seen him, and the one speaking with you is he." He said, "Lord, I believe." And he worshipped him. Jesus said, "I came into this world for judgment so that those who do not see may see, and those who do see may become blind." Some of the Pharisees near him heard this and said to him, "Surely we are not blind, are we?" Jesus said to them, "If you were blind, you would not have sin. But now that you say, 'We see,' your sin remains." (NRSV)

Learning to See

Joseph S. Pagano

During Lent this year, I am reading Dante's *Divine Comedy*. As many of you know, the *Divine Comedy* is made up of three parts: *The Inferno*, *Purgatory*, and *Paradise*. Right now I am in the middle of *Purgatory* and I don't know if I am going to make it to *Paradise* by Easter. I hope so! I don't want to get bogged down and end up stuck somewhere between the *slothful* and the *avaricious*.

It is a wonderful poem to read during Lent because it is about a journey whose final destination is God. One of the central motifs in the journey is the interplay between darkness and light. God is described as the Eternal Light, and the goal of the journey is to see the Eternal Light, face to face in the beatific vision. Dante's description of the beatific vision is one of the most famous and beautiful in all of literature. He writes, "O grace abounding and allowing me to dare / to fix my gaze on the Eternal Light, / so deep my vision was consumed in It! / I saw how it contains within its depths / all things bound in a single book by love / of which creation is the scattered leaves."[4] It is a beautiful and radiant description of the goal of the spiritual life. However, before he can get there, the Pilgrim must first travel through the Inferno and Purgatory, and this is a journey from darkness to light. Hell, as the negation of the Eternal Light, is all darkness, and when the Pilgrim finally makes it out of the Inferno, his eyes need to adjust to seeing in the light again. In a passage from Purgatory, the Pilgrim is stunned by the intensity of an angelic light and he needs to shield his eyes. Dante writes, "suddenly I felt my brow forced down / by a light far brighter than I sensed before; / my mind was stunned by what it did not know. / I placed both of my hands above my eyes / and used them as a visor for my face / to temper the intensity of light."[5] Learning to see can be a painful process. But the Pilgrim is reassured by his guide that at some point "not long from now, a sight like this will prove / to be no burden, but a joy as great / as Nature has prepared your soul to feel."[6] What is painful to behold now, will someday be looked upon with great joy.

Dante writes with great insight into the spiritual journey. It is not simply a movement from total blindness to complete vision, from abject misery to total joy. It is a more complicated, and, often times, a more painful process. The spiritual journey is more like regaining one's sight in stages, and, initially, regaining one's sight can be painful and confusing. As we grow spiritually, we may become aware of truths about ourselves and our world that may be difficult to look upon. Looking honestly at the

---

4. Dante, *Paradiso* XXXIII, 82–87.
5. Dante, *Purgatorio*, XV, 10–15.
6. Dante, *Purgatorio*, XV, 31–33.

pettiness and prejudice in our lives is not an easy thing to do. And yet, the promise is that this is not the end of the story, this is not the end of the journey. The promise is that through this process our sight is becoming stronger, and that, someday, we will see all these things as part of God's great love story; we will see the "Eternal Light that contains within its depths all things bound in a single book by love."

I mention Dante's vision of the spiritual journey because I think it is more true and more realistic than the snappier version that says, "I once was lost, but now am found, was blind but now I see." You know the words, "Amazing grace, how sweet the sound that saved a wretch like me, I once was lost, but now am found, was blind, but now I see." We love that story. I love that story. We love dramatic stories about people turning their lives around in a flash. Maybe that's why I like country music so much, especially Hank Williams. You know how the story goes. Something like "I was a lyin', cheatin', low-down, sneakin' around, double-dealin', drinkin', miserable excuse for a human bein', driving my pick-up down the road of perdition. But then God took the wheel and turned me around, and like the blind man that got back his sight, praise Jesus, I saw the light. Now I'm on the straight and narrow, come out of the tunnel of darkness, and there's nothing but blue skies ahead. Praise the Lord, I saw the light!" It's a catchy story, a riff on "I once was lost, but now am found, was blind, but now I see." But, as you may or may not know, it wasn't true for Hank Williams. Williams had a terribly troubled life and he died tragically at the age of twenty-nine. And, as you may or may not know, it wasn't true for John Newton, who wrote the hymn "Amazing Grace," either. Newton was a former slave-ship captain who had a conversion experience and later became an Anglican clergyman. But he did not immediately denounce the slave trade and become an abolitionist. He came to that later in life, under the influence of William Wilberforce, and ultimately of God's grace. The working of God's grace in Newton's life was more like a process of growing in insight and vision than the "all at once" switch from total blindness to total sight implied in his famous hymn. It seems the spiritual journey is like a process of regaining one's sight, which can be difficult and painful.

In our Gospel lesson for today, we hear the story of the healing of the man who was born blind. The story is the biblical source for the hymn "Amazing Grace." But it is actually a very different story than the one told in "Amazing Grace." Even in the highly symbolic world of John, our gospels are always more realistic than our pious representations of them.

Because the story isn't about a man whose life was terrible because he was blind, and then he was healed and gained his sight and everything was peachy keen. Actually, it's just the other way around, because in the story, it is really after the man gets his sight that his trouble begins. After he regains his sight, he is questioned by his neighbors, he is berated by the religious authorities, and he is ultimately expelled from the community. He was a lot better off when he was blind. It is after he gains his sight that all hell breaks loose. At one point, when he is being cross-examined by the authorities, he says in exasperation, "All I know is this: I was blind, but now I see." This is not a happy statement. It is the statement of a man who has seen and experienced the realities of human prejudice and persecution. He has gained his sight and what he sees are the fears and hatreds of people who will ultimately cast him out. As John tells us, the religious authorities said to him, "You were born totally in sin, and are you trying to teach us?" Then they threw him out. It is after the blind man begins to see that his troubles really begin. People lie about him, and demean him, and then the throw him out. Regaining one's sight can be a painful process.

The spiritual truth expressed in this story is that learning to see can be a complicated and painful process. And, I think, deep down, we all know this. One of the things I always ask people is, "How is your spiritual life going?" I get a variety of answers to this question, but one of the most frequent responses I get is "I just can't go there right now." Sometimes, it is either too painful or too confusing to confront the reality of our lives. Better to keep rushing around from one thing to another, than to sit down and examine our lives. Better to keep trying to climb the next rung of the ladder, than to think about whether we have been scaling the wrong wall. Better to go through life with blinders on, than to see the reality of the world around us and within us. Learning to see the truth about ourselves and the truth about our world can be a painful and confusing process.

But even though it can be painful to gain spiritual insight, this is not the end of the story. There really is amazing grace. It may not be as sudden as John Newton suggests, but there is grace for the journey. It may be painful to see the truth about ourselves, but the promise is that this is only a stop on a journey whose final destination is God. And God is the Eternal Light that contains within its depths all things bound in a single book by love. Yes, it is true that we are petty and proud creatures. We do live in a world that has too much fear and prejudice. This is true and it is painful to look at honestly. But, the deeper truth, the truth that beats at the heart of the universe, is that we are each of us the beloved children of God, and that this world of ours is the beloved creation of God. Real sight, the vision of God, is the vision of the Love that moves the sun and the other stars, the love that created you and me and everything that exists, the Love that longs to bring all things back into harmony and union with itself. It is this Love, it is this promise, that gives us the courage to look at our lives and our world truly. Learning to see, to look at the reality of our lives may be a painful process. But this is not the end of the story, this is only a part of the journey. The journey's final destination is God and God is Love. In loving union with God we realize that despite our weaknesses and blindness, we are all God's beloved children, that despite its brokenness and pain, this is God's beloved creation.

In the beginning of John's Gospel, Jesus is referred to as "the true light which enlightens everyone." Having caught a glimpse of this light, we turn toward him as plants turn toward the sun. The light of creation overcoming the darkness of destruction; the light of truth overcoming the darkness of error; the light of peace overcoming the darkness of strife; the light of life overcoming the darkness of death; the light of love overcoming the darkness of hatred. This light, this love, this promise gives us the courage to look at ourselves and our world. Learning to see can be a painful process. But the promise is that beyond the pain and confusion, there is grace, amazing grace. There is love, the Love that moves the sun and the other stars, the Love that flung the galaxies and thought up butterflies, the Love that created you and me and longs to bring us home.

20/20 Vision

Amy Richter

Now that I am firmly in my forties, it's happening just like the eye doctor told me it would. First, a little more than a year ago, following some feelings of eyestrain and fatigue, I was fitted for my first pair of reading glasses. Having enjoyed the blessing of great eyesight for forty-plus years, I was initially dismayed at having to remember to wear my glasses. But I also experienced the wonder of the difference eye glasses make: no more headaches! Bright colors! Clear words! Why did I wait so long?

It's about time for my next check up and I think my eyes are getting worse. It's probably time for graduated lenses. I notice it is getting more difficult to switch from looking at the congregation to the altar book, for example, to the chalice and paten on the altar, and back again. But rather than fear the change, this time I'm ready, looking forward to the increased clarity. Why wouldn't I want to see all these precious sights—you, the sacramental vessels, the words of our liturgy—in all their beauty?

I have noticed, however, one entertaining aspect of my pre-corrected worsening vision: the way my imagination jumps in when I don't see quite clearly. For example, when I ride my bike through the park, my eye will catch a glimpse of something I can't quite make out and my imagination fills in. What at first glance appears to be an exceptionally large tortoise turns out to be a rock. Was that a crouching panther? Nope—tree stump. A large bird preening itself is, in actuality, a large bush with a protruding branch. What appears to be the case given a passing glance, under closer, clearer investigation, turns out to be something different.

While the opportunity to exercise my imagination is sometimes enjoyable, other times it is not. Tree roots can appear to be snakes. Blowing leaves can look like really large insects. I have jumped away from too many fearsome things that turned out to be mere figments of my imagination. Passing glances are not good enough.

This is true in our faith lives as well. Do we give the foundations of our faith more than a passing glance? Are we using lenses that distort rather than correct our vision?

Sometimes people have images of God or beliefs about the Christian faith or Christians that may be fanciful, flimsy, or maybe even frightening—misconceptions based on a passing glance, but won't turn out to be true when examined more deeply.

In today's Gospel we see a whole group of people who may, in fact, have 20/20 vision, but not see things as they really are.

Jesus sees a man blind from birth. His disciples, however, see a theological conundrum. A man is blind. Whose sin caused this? The man's sins? Or was it something his parents did? The disciples suffer from a kind of spiritual vision problem. They accept a folk theology that says if there is something wrong with you, or if you're suffering from some illness, it must be because of sin—yours, or maybe your parents'.

We still hear that kind of thinking when people say that illness is God's punishment, or that God causes suffering because people have sinned in some way. People do sin, and sometimes our actions have negative consequences for our health and well-being. Behavior that is not life-giving or healthy, behavior that is risky or dangerous or unwholesome can certainly have a negative impact on our health.

But Jesus says the man's blindness was not the result of sin. God didn't strike him with blindness because of someone's sin. God doesn't work like that. But God can bring good out of a bad situation. God does bring light out of darkness. God can be glorified despite hardship and suffering. Look, Jesus says to the disciples. Look again. Look closely. You saw a snake. It's really a stick. You saw guilt and blame. It's really an opportunity to see God do something beautiful.

Jesus cures the man born blind. For the first time in his life the man is able to see.

You would think that such a happy event would be the cause for some community rejoicing, celebration. But, no, other vision problems get in the way. What should make people very happy for the man leads to controversy and confusion about what's right before their eyes.

The man's neighbors aren't sure they're seeing the same man. It looks like him, but maybe it's someone else. You can imagine the neighborhood squabble: yes, it's him. No, it's not. Is too. Is not. Meanwhile, the man is jumping up and down, waving his arms and saying, "It's me! It's really me!" It's as if the neighbors are wearing dark glasses that keep them from seeing the joy of this man who can see for the first time in his life. It's as if they're wearing sunglasses that, instead of UV ray filters, have miracle filters. They just can't see it.

The disciples need corrective lenses for their theology. The man's neighbors need to take off their good news-blocking sunglasses. And the Pharisees also suffer from some serious vision problems.

The Pharisees are blinded by their adherence to the Sabbath law. It is as if they wear the law like a blindfold. So tightly are they wrapped up in the rules, that they can't see the grace and mercy of God before them in Jesus. They don't care that the man can now see. All they can see is that Jesus broke the Sabbath laws by making clay and by healing a man whose illness wasn't life threatening on the Sabbath. When glancing at Jesus, they see a sinner. They can't see the wonderful things Jesus is doing.

The one person who ends up with clear vision and a life-giving outlook is the man born blind, who by the end of the story comes to new levels of spiritual insight about Jesus. When the man who can now see is thrown out, excluded from the community, Jesus comes to him. Jesus will not let him be cast out. Jesus finds him and reveals to him that Jesus is the Son of Man, the one who has come into the world to heal and seek and save the lost. Jesus is the light of the world. And by his light, the man once blind can see light.

What about us? Perhaps we are like the disciples and need some corrective lenses for how we think about God. Perhaps we are like the neighbors and wear dark glasses that block out the powerful rays of joy, the rays of the possibility of really great things happening right in our midst. Perhaps we are like the Pharisees who wear our rules, our ways of thinking about how things should be, the ways things have always been done, the only right way to do things, like a blindfold that keeps us from seeing new possibilities for service, keeps us from seeing the people we are meant to serve. Perhaps we have some other blind spot that keeps us from fully knowing Jesus as the light of the world. Perhaps we are content to give Jesus and faith only a passing glance, even if what we see there is merely our imagination filling in the great big gaps in our perception.

Lent is a time to let Jesus examine our vision and heal our blind spots. Let Jesus open our eyes to deeper insights. Tell Jesus what you have trouble seeing, what it is about him or the world or your neighbors or yourself that is unclear to you. Let him correct your vision and adjust your outlook. He may give you exercises to do, like prayer and reading. He may give you people to spend time with, people to welcome, include, and serve, people in whom we can see God doing good things, people with whom to rejoice in our God-given blessings, people to recognize and celebrate as neighbors and friends, people who are valued and redeemed and loved by God. Jesus may challenge the notion that seeing is believing and tell you instead that believing is what makes us able to see. There is much that we can see only after we have begun to believe, only after we have allowed hope to be nurtured in us through faith. He will certainly invite you to partake of his supper, the Eucharistic feast, in which appearances can be deceiving, but with the eyes of faith we can see that a piece of bread and a sip of wine are a banquet, and the foretaste of heavenly feast to come.

May we let Jesus, the light of the world, touch our sight, give us vision and life-giving outlook that by his light, we may see light.

5

Triumphant Love—Sermons for Easter

EASTER DAY YEAR B

Mark 16:1–8

When the sabbath was over, Mary Magdalene, and Mary the mother of James, and Salome bought spices, so that they might go and anoint him. And very early on the first day of the week, when the sun had risen, they went to the tomb. They had been saying to one another, "Who will roll away the stone for us from the entrance to the tomb?" When they looked up, they saw that the stone, which was very large, had already been rolled back. As they entered the tomb, they saw a young man, dressed in a white robe, sitting on the right side; and they were alarmed. But he said to them, "Do not be alarmed; you are looking for Jesus of Nazareth, who was crucified. He has been raised; he is not here. Look, there is the place they laid him. But go, tell his disciples and Peter that he is going ahead of you to Galilee; there you will see him, just as he told you." So they went out and fled from the tomb, for terror and amazement had seized them; and they said nothing to anyone, for they were afraid. (NRSV)

Let Him Easter in Us

Joseph S. Pagano

Gerard Manley Hopkins has a wonderful poem, "The Wreck of the Deutschland," where he uses the phrase "Let him easter in us." In this phrase, he uses the noun "Easter" as a verb. Hopkins writes, "Let him easter in us, be a dayspring to the dimness of us."[1] It is a splendid phrase. It is a beautiful prayer really, "Let him easter in us." In fact, I think this is a great way to look at the real truth, the transforming reality of Easter. Let Easter get into us. Let Easter come and live where we live. Let Easter permeate our souls. Let him Easter in us, and be a dayspring to the dimness of us.

Isn't that really what we all desire most? Not Easter as a noun, about a long-ago event. But, rather, Easter as a verb, as something that transforms our present lives, as something that gives us new life now, as something that gives us hope and meaning and courage. Isn't that what every human heart longs for? Let him Easter in us!

Phillips Brooks, a 19th century Bishop of Massachusetts, once talked about the truth of Easter as "the truth of the new man for the new world, the regeneration for and by the resurrection." He says, "That, be assured, is the great Easter truth. Not that we are to live newly after death—that is not the great thing—but that we are to be new here and now by the power of the resurrection; not so much that we are to live forever as that we are to, and may, live nobly now because we are to live forever."[2] The good news of Easter is that there is the possibility of new life now. The power of the resurrection is not something that simply awaits us after death, but something that also comes to us now, that comes to us always, that proclaims the good news that new life is possible here, now, today.

It does seem like in so many ways, people are longing for an experience of Easter in their lives. A widow whose husband died at a much too early age. A man who is struggling with a new career at midlife and fears his ability to cope with new challenges. A colleague who fell into a deep, clinical depression and struggles to live through the day with meager energy. In so many ways, so many people are longing for new life, for God to Easter in us, and be a dayspring to the dimness of us.

1. Gardner and MacKenzie, *The Poems of Gerard Manley Hopkins*, 63.
2. Brooks, *Sermons*, 279–280.

A Man, A Woman, A Word of Love

I suppose one could say that the women who arrived at the tomb early on that first Easter morning also needed to experience Easter as a verb. Look at how the Gospel of Mark tells it. The women came to the tomb thinking that the story had ended, that it was all over between them and Jesus. They had gone to attend to the dead body of Jesus, to anoint him, to wrap him up, and to give him a proper burial, and, we may suppose, to mourn the loss of their Lord. What they get when they arrive is a breathtaking announcement that God has raised Christ from the dead and that he has gone ahead of them to Galilee where they will see him. What they get is Easter as a noun, and we have no reason to believe that they doubted that God had, in fact, raised Christ from the dead. It's just that the reality of the event was so overwhelming that they were dumbfounded. As Mark says, "they went out and fled the tomb, for terror and amazement had seized them; and they said nothing to anyone, for they were afraid." They experienced Easter as a noun, but they had not yet experienced Easter as a verb because they said nothing to anyone, for they were afraid.

Our other Gospels tell us that the women eventually did experience Easter as a verb because they did eventually go and tell the other disciples that Christ had been raised from the dead. He Eastered in them and they were transformed from a group of terrified people who were frightened and fearful, to apostles, to people who boldly go forth from the tomb and proclaim the good news that because Christ is risen life is stronger than death, love is stronger than hate, and God's peace is more powerful than human violence.

Let him Easter in us, and be a dayspring to the dimness of us. Easter is a verb. It is something that happens to us. Easter is true when it lives where we live, and permeates our souls.

A few years ago, John Dominic Crossan and N. T. Wright engaged in a public dialogue on the meaning of the resurrection. As one might expect with two scholars from different ends of the theological spectrum, they expressed some sharp differences on how they understood the nature of the resurrection. But, rather surprisingly, they both agreed on one thing: that the real meaning of the early Christian witness to the resurrection was about the transformation of our lives and our world right now. Bishop Wright puts it this way: "Those of you who are going to preach on Easter Sunday, please note that the resurrection stories in the Gospels do not say Jesus is raised, therefore we're going to heaven or therefore we're going to be raised. They say Jesus is raised, therefore, God's new creation has begun and we've got a job to do."[3] Crossan says that the resurrection means "that God's Great Clean-Up of a world grown old in evil and impurity, injustice and violence has already begun . . . and we are called to participate in it."[4] He adds, "The end of the world is not what we are talking about. We're talking about cosmic transformation of this world."[5] Now, when two New Testament scholars with as widely divergent as views as Wright and Crossan agree on something we should take notice. The great Easter truth is not that we are simply to live newly after death, but that we are to be new, here and now, by the power of the resurrection.

Jim Wallis tells a story that strikes me as a resurrection story. At least, it is if we take seriously what Bishop Wright says about the resurrection's meaning that God's new creation has begun and our call to participate in it. Wallis was in South Africa at a time when Nelson Mandela was still in prison and when apartheid still ruled the land. Wallis was at a worship service at the Cathedral of St. George's where Archbishop Desmond Tutu was presiding, when a group of the notorious South African Security Police broke into the service. Wallis writes, "Tutu stopped preaching and just looked at the intruders as they lined the walls of his cathedral, wielding writing pads and tape recorders to record whatever he said and thereby threatening him with consequences for any bold prophetic utterances. They had already arrested Tutu and other church leaders just a few weeks before and kept them in jail for several days." Wallis continues, "After meeting their eyes with his in a steely gaze, [Tutu] acknowledged their power . . . but reminded them that he served a higher power than their political authority . . . Then, in the most extraordinary challenge to political tyranny I have ever witnessed, Archbishop Desmond Tutu told the representatives of South African Apartheid, 'Since you have already lost, I invite you today to come and join the winning side!' He said it with a smile on his face and enticing warmth in his invitation, but with a clarity and a boldness that took everyone's breath away. The congregation's response was electric. The crowd was literally transformed by the bishop's challenge to power. From a cowering fear of the heavily armed security forces that surrounded the cathedral and greatly outnumbered the band

---

3. Wright and Crossan, "The Resurrection: Historical Event or Theological Explanation? A Dialogue," 21.

4. Crossan, "Appendix: Bodily-Resurrection Faith," 186.

5. Wright and Crossan, 25.

of worshippers, we literally leaped to our feet, shouted the praises of God and began . . . dancing . . .We danced out of the cathedral to meet the awaiting police and military forces of apartheid who hardly expected a confrontation with dancing worshippers. Not knowing what else to do, they backed up to provide the space for the people of faith to dance for freedom in the streets of South Africa."[6]

Ten years later, Wallis attended the inauguration of Nelson Mandela as president. Wallis spoke to Archbishop Tutu and asked him if he remembered that earlier day when they had danced out of the Cathedral onto the streets, and Tutu said that, indeed, he did. Wallis reflects that apartheid did not die on the day Mandela was released or inaugurated, but that it died the day of the celebration in the church, when they danced for freedom in the streets of South Africa. Wallis adds that it was Tutu's deeply held Christian belief and in particular his belief in the resurrection that kept him going in the dark days of apartheid.

Easter is something that happens in us. Easter is a verb. The good news of Easter is not simply that God has raised Christ from the dead. The good news of Easter is also about the possibility and the promise that new life is available to each one of us here and now. God has raised Christ from the dead and we can claim this new life and make it our own. Right now, at this moment, we can let go of past hurts and grudges, and start over. Right here, right now, we can overcome our fear and fixation on death and trust in the Lord of life and love. Right here, right now, wherever we are, we can claim new life in our families, in our jobs, in our relationships, in our churches, in this broken but beautiful world. We can be new "here and now by the power of the resurrection." God's "Great Clean Up of the world" has begun, and we can joyfully participate. We can let Easter get into us; let Easter come and live where we live; let Easter permeate our souls. We can let him Easter in us, and be a dayspring to the dimness of us.

Alleluia! Christ is risen. The Lord is risen indeed. Alleluia!

---

6. Wallis, *God's Politics*, 347–48.

Set Free from the Stone

Amy Richter

A few years ago, Joe and I spent time in the city of Florence in Italy. On our list of must-see attractions was the Academy Gallery, home to many important works of art.

In one hall we saw an almost 9-foot tall block of white marble. The figure of a man half-emerges from the stone block from which he was being carved, but which still imprisons him. The figure is Saint Matthew, the Gospel writer. Crooked in his left arm is his Gospel book. His bearded face turns slightly upward and to the right as his torso twists in the opposite direction. His left knee protrudes closest to the viewer, his thigh muscles taut as if he is trying to pull his foot, still submerged in the stone, free. There is so much energy in his body, muscles taut and twisting, that he practically writhes to get loose from the stone. He looks like if he relaxes for a moment, the stone will simply swallow him back up and he will be trapped forever. But his struggle for freedom from the stone is in vain. It would take an act from a power outside to wrest him free, and his creator, the artist who tried valiantly to liberate him, finally decided he could not do it and gave up.

The artist is Michelangelo Buonarroti, and it's no accident that St. Matthew looks like he was abandoned half-way through the stone cutting. Michelangelo had the ability to see in a block of stone a sculpture within, a figure within the stone that he knew he could—with care and precision and focused vision—set free. Michelangelo described his work as "liberating the figure from the marble that imprisons it."[7] Art historian H. W. Janson wrote of Michelangelo, "Only the 'liberation' of real, three-dimensional bodies from recalcitrant matter could satisfy his urge."[8] Janson says, "We may believe he could see 'isolated signs of life' within the marble—a knee or an elbow pressing against the surface." He usually made many drawings and sometimes small models "before he dared assault the 'marble prison' itself, for that, he knew, was the final contest between him and his material. Once he started carving, every stroke of the chisel would commit him more and more to a specific conception of

---

7. Janson, *History of Art*, 12.
8. Ibid., 424.

the figure hidden in the block, and the marble would permit him to free the figure whole only if his guess as to its shape was correct."[9]

Sometimes Michelangelo didn't guess right and gave up, like he did with St. Matthew. But that, of course, is not the Michelangelo sculpture we went to the Academy to see.

We had gone to see Michelangelo's masterpiece, his David. And if you have seen it, then you too have marveled at how an artist could make cold white marble look like a flesh and blood man. It's breathtaking: the nearly 14-foot high statue of David, shepherd and future king of Israel, set free by the artist's vision and hand from a huge block of white Carrara marble.

David stands, gazing outward, not aggressive, but watchful. Over his left shoulder he holds his slingshot. In his right hand is one of the five smooth stones that were his improbable weapon against the giant Philistine soldier, enemy of David's people. Goliath had roared with laughter when he saw the shepherd boy approach with his tiny projectiles. His laugh was cut short when David let just one small stone fly and it struck the giant square in the forehead and killed him. No, David is not worried, not afraid. He knows that God told him he would be victorious. He is not anxious. But his eyes are wide open.

Somehow Michelangelo could see in a slab of marble what others could not. Others had tried with that very same block of marble, a six-ton block so large and imposing it was nicknamed "the Giant." When the block had first been hauled to Florence, an artist named Agostino di Duccio was hired to sculpt a David from it to be placed on the roof of the cathedral.[10] Agostino gave up after some preliminary work on the legs. Ten years later the commission was give to an artist named Rossellino who made no further progress and lost the commission after a few years. Twenty-five years after the block of stone was first dragged to Florence, the job was given to Michelangelo, just 26 years old at the time.[11] For the next three years, he kept his eyes on the marble, and worked carefully, diligently, deliberately to bring David forth from the stone.[12] After three years, David was free, and Michelangelo's work endures to this day.

---

9. Ibid., 12.
10. S. Bietoletti et al., *Florence*, 344.
11. Janson, 425.
12. The David was completed in 1504. Ibid., 424.

Triumphant Love—Sermons for Easter

On that first Easter morning, a group of women, faithful followers of Jesus came to his tomb expecting to see stone—and lots of it. The dead body of their Lord had been placed in a tomb hewn from rock and a large stone had been rolled in front of it. The corpse of Jesus was encased in stone, not because anyone expected anything to come out of the tomb, but to prevent people and animals from getting at the body. It was a way to revere and respect a corpse, to preserve it, let it rest in peace.

But the women came with their own way to revere the body. The women had brought spices to anoint their friend's corpse in its tomb. They were expecting to see a stone, and the stone was a problem, especially the heavy stone sealing the tomb shut. They knew that the stone was a problem and they were trying to solve it.

But then these three women do something that will change their lives forever. They "look up." The word can also mean they "looked again." And what they saw when they looked up, when they looked again, when they really saw what was actually before them, was that the stone had already been rolled back. God had already solved the problem. The stone was not an impediment. They were not trapped on the outside wondering how to get in.

But, more astonishingly so, nor was anyone trapped inside. The women go into the tomb and they see a young man, dressed in a white robe, sitting on the right side of where Jesus' corpse should have been. But the body isn't there. The white-robed messenger tells them, "You are looking for Jesus of Nazareth, who was crucified. He has been raised; he is not here. Look . . . he has already gone on ahead of you to Galilee. You go there now too. You will see him there."

The stone is no impediment. The Creator, Almighty, Eternal God who made life in the beginning, now brings new life. The Creator reaches into the stone and brings out, not a lifeless statue, but a living, glorious, resurrected Son, Jesus Christ. The tombstone now signals triumph.

"Jesus has been raised. He has already gone on ahead of you to Galilee. You will see him there. Go!"

Stone is such a good metaphor for human existence. It expresses permanence and our desire that something of ourselves remain after we're gone. But stone's permanence—unyielding, unmoving, unchanging—is also why stone is such a good metaphor for fear, that human emotion, response that can paralyze us, keep us frozen, petrified, as if turned to stone. It's such a good metaphor for the ways we let habits and expectations weigh us down and keep us from being brave enough to follow where God leads us, from trusting that God wants goodness and new life for us, abundant life known through love of God and neighbor, in this life now.

God is still in the stone moving business, still chiseling away at whatever stone imprisons us, still rolling heavy rocks away, still filing, chipping, hammering—whatever is necessary to bring trapped people out from what binds us to unhealthy, deadening, or fearful places, to what petrifies us and keeps us stuck, even if we're busy fleeing rather than following. God's raising of Jesus means that no tomb will hold us in death. But no stone-like prison needs to hold us in this life either. God, our creator, reaches toward us and invites us into freedom, new life, even now. Jesus Christ, will meet us wherever we are, even if we are trapped in a situation akin to a lifeless, airless, stone tomb. He is willing to be with us there. But he would rather bring us out into the sunshine and fresh air. The invitation is always to step forth, to go and meet him, to follow him on the way, not stay back in the tomb.

Is there a stone weighing you down? Some stone in which you are imbedded? Some tombstone you are carrying around with you? Are you busy fleeing from some fear, confused because you are moving so fast, why does it feel you're not getting anywhere? God wants to give us all new life, pull us out from the rock, set us free. We can't do it ourselves. It takes a power from outside, an artist, a true Creator, who can see us for everything we can be, and wants to set us free for new life now.

Need some stone moved? God can do it. And what comes out will be so beautiful.

6

Transforming Love—Sermons for the Sundays after Pentecost

PROPER 14, YEAR B

John 6:35, 48–51

Jesus said to them, "I am the bread of life. Whoever comes to me will never be hungry, and whoever believes in me will never be thirsty . . . I am the bread of life. Your ancestors ate the manna in the wilderness, and they died. This is the bread that comes down from heaven, so that one may eat of it and not die. I am the living bread that came down from heaven. Whoever eats of this bread will live for ever; and the bread that I will give for the life of the world is my flesh." (NRSV)

Bread of Life

Joseph S. Pagano

I know what heaven smells like. The Italian Peoples Bakery. When I was a little boy my grandmother and I would walk to the bakery early in the morning, just as it was opening for business. She held my hand as we walked along streets sided by the neat row-homes of Chambersburg, the Little Italy section of Trenton, New Jersey. I can still see the red, white and green awnings of the Italian Peoples Bakery, I can still hear the jingle of the bell as the front door opened for business, and I can still smell the aroma of fresh bread pouring into the streets. Inside, I remember the heat from the huge ovens warming my face as I looked at the loaves inside turning a crispy brown. But most of all I remember inhaling the sweet barley smell of fresh bread. Holding my grandmother's hand in the Italian Peoples Bakery and smelling the freshly baked bread was like heaven.

In my Italian family we didn't just smell the bread. We ate it. Right away. While it was still hot. When we got back to my grandmother's place, she would pull out a stick of butter, real butter that is, sliced open the loaf, and then we would eat hot, fresh bread with huge chucks of butter melting into it. It tasted like heaven.

I know that there are some well-known diets that tell us to lay off the bread. I'm sure there are scientific studies showing why avoiding bread in your diet makes sense. But, in my heart of hearts, I just can't believe it. As an Italian American kid from New Jersey I just can't make myself believe that eating bread can be bad for you. I can't imagine life without bread.

Jerre Mangione and Ben Morreale talk of the importance of bread for southern Italians, the folks that made up about ninety percent of the Italians who emigrated to America. They say, "For most southern Italians their sturdy bread was the mainstay. When cutting a new loaf, one would make the sign of the cross on its level side and kiss the knife before cutting into it. One would never set the bread on its rounded side: bread was respected. A good man was said to be as good as 'a piece of bread.'"[1] Not good as gold as we say in this country. But as good as bread!

We see something of this bread-like virtue in our word "companion," which literally means someone with whom bread is shared: *com*, meaning "with," and *pani*, meaning "bread." A *com-panion* is someone with whom we break bread. And when we break bread with someone, we are in communion with them. The literary critic Thomas Foster says this about breaking bread: "Here's the thing to remember about communion of all kinds: in the real world, breaking bread together is an act of sharing and peace, since if you're breaking bread you're not breaking heads." Foster continues, "We're quite particular about those with whom we break

---

1. Mangione and Morreale, *La Storia*, 38.

bread. We may not, for instance, accept a dinner invitation from someone we don't care for. The act of taking food into our bodies is so personal that we really only want to do it with people we're very comfortable with . . . Generally, eating with another is a way of saying, 'I'm with you, I like you, we form a community together.' And that is a form of communion."[2]

In our Gospel lesson for today, Jesus says he is the bread of heaven. He says, "I am the bread of life. Your ancestors ate the manna in the wilderness and they died. This is the bread that comes down from heaven, so that one may eat of it and not die. I am the living bread that came down from heaven."

In this passage, Jesus contrasts his life-giving bread with the Old Testament story of manna in the wilderness. In this story, the Israelites had been freed from their bondage in Egypt and were on their way to the Promised Land. But before they entered the Promised Land, they had to wander for many years in the desert. During this time they were sustained by God's gift of manna, a flakey, bread-like substance that God provided for them daily. But, as Jesus points out, while manna was food for the journey, it wasn't the same thing as the bread of life, because even though they ate it, they died. What Jesus is saying is that through him, in him, God is providing a different type of food, for a different type of journey. In Christ, God is providing the bread of life. This is food for our journey out of error into truth, out of sin into righteousness, out of death into life. Jesus is food for our journey into the true promised land of eternal life with God.

It's an extraordinary promise. Jesus is not only our companion on the way, the one with whom we break bread, but he is also the bread itself, the bread that came down from heaven to give us eternal life. No doubt Jesus is our companion. He is our brother, our teacher, our friend. But in our Gospel lesson for this morning, Jesus is saying that he is all this and more. He is the one who has come to give us life and give it abundantly. In him was life and the life was the light of all people. He is the bread of life.

When we gather together for the Holy Eucharist, we catch a glimpse of the heavenly life that Jesus promises us. The Eucharist is that sacrament whereby we get a foretaste of that heavenly banquet when all things will be put to rights, when all hurts will be mended, when all tears will be wiped away, when all divisions will be repaired, when God will be all in

---

2. Foster, *How to Read Literature*, 8.

all. This is why we call it Holy Communion. It is a holy union with God and with all of creation in relationship to God. And one of the things that distinguishes this breaking of bread from so many other meals is that everyone is welcome. The high and mighty and the lowly and humble; friends and enemies; relatives and strangers. All of God's children are welcome at God's table. All are companions, all are people we break bread with, because Christ himself is the bread that has been broken and the blood that has been poured out for the life and salvation of the whole world.

In one of our communion prayers we say, "Deliver us from the presumption of coming to this table for solace only, and not for strength; for pardon only, and not for renewal. Let the grace of this Holy Communion make us one body, one spirit in Christ, that we may worthily serve the world in his name." We share the bread of life so that we may be strengthened and renewed to go forth into the word with a message of life and love. In small and large ways, sharing in the bread of life, sharing in Christ's love, transforms us and our world.

Stephanie Paulsell tells a story about the transformative power of Holy Communion. Diana Ventura was in seminary where she was learning to be an ordained minister. She was an exceptionally good student: smart, compassionate, and funny. But before she began her year of supervised ministry in a parish setting, she became very anxious. Ventura had been born with cerebral palsy, which caused her to jerk a bit when she walked and to drag one leg, and she was terribly afraid that she would spill the cup on the floor or even worse on someone she was serving. But the time came for her to serve and she gave it a try and things went well. No spills. She made it through her duty. Then, Paulsell writes, "one spring Sunday, Diana served again as cupbearer and walked from person to person kneeling at the rail at the front of her church, offering them a drink. 'The blood of Christ,' she said to each one, 'the cup of salvation.' And as she raised the cup to each person's lips, taking the utmost care not to fall, she saw her own reflection in the shiny silver chalice. Over and over again, she saw the reflection of her body in the cup. This is my broken body, she thought, serving this church. This is my body teaching people what we do with brokenness in the church. Here in this cup is new life, and here is my body, expressing the truth of what this new life means!"[3]

---

3. Paulsell, *Honoring the Body*, 110–111.

Jesus said, "I am the bread of life. Whoever comes to me will never be hungry, and whoever believes in me will never be thirsty . . . And this is the will of him who sent me, that I should lose nothing of all that he has given me, but raise it up on the last day." In the bread of life, our souls are blessed and nourished. In the bread of life, nothing is lost, not even our brokenness. In the bread of life, we are raised to eternal life. The bread of life is the bread from heaven.

The Meaning of Pie and Other Holy Mysteries

Amy Richter

The first summer after my mother died, a woman from my father's church asked if she could come over and pick raspberries from the bushes she knew that Mom and Dad had grown from the spindly canes that came from the mail order catalogue into thick healthy shrubs laden with fruit. The woman was one of the elders of the church, an older woman, plump with white hair always pulled back. She wore sensible beige shoes with rubber soles and Velcro straps, and, whenever I had seen her, light blue slacks and a flowered print shirt. She had served her time in the Sunday School and the choir, the crafters group, and the altar guild. But her love was baking.

She said to my father, "They have to be picked, if you want them to keep producing. And I want to make you a pie. You don't get raspberry often because it takes a whole lot of berries and you have a whole bunch of berries just waiting to be made into pie." She picked the berries on a sunny July morning when the sun was starting to evaporate the dew off the grass and the leaves, and returned in the afternoon with the pie: homemade crust, red raspberries and filling peeking through the golden brown lattice criss-crossing the top, and still warm.

"Enjoy a piece with me?" my dad asked. "I can't eat an entire pie by myself." He poured them each a glass of 2% milk and cut two pieces of the pie. It was marvelous—sweet, tart, gooey delicious fruit. Flaky, tender, slightly salty crust. Perfect, especially with the milk to wash it down and clear the palate for the next bite. He thanked her for the pie.

Although the pie would have been a luxurious treat—he could certainly have enjoyed it piece by piece by himself—he got an idea. He packed up the pie and took it with him when he went to make a pastoral visit he had scheduled that day.

"Here, have a piece of pie," he said. He sliced a piece and dished it onto one of the paper plates he had brought along. "I won't stay long, but I think you will enjoy this."

They visited while the parishioner ate the pie, a small piece, enough to taste, but the richness of the sweet and tart and tender made a small piece just the right amount.

He thought next of who might actually not just enjoy a piece of the pie, but need the pie; who might need some simple pleasure: some tangible reminder that unassuming things like berries and sugar, flour and salt can be transformed into something that lets you actually taste summer in a mouthful; who might be served by this undemanding manifestation of care and love in edible form.

The pie was too good not to share. He spent the rest of the day sharing the pie, slice by modest slice. He and those with whom he shared it found that even a small piece could convey the essence of it: sunshine, earth, abundance, creativity, compassion.

He came to think of it as communion by pie, a kind of grace that conveyed the knowledge that he was part of a larger community and that connection was part of what he hungered for. The pie did not cause the connection, of course. But the pie was the means for it: a way to say, I see you. I want you to join me in enjoyment, in nourishment, in a moment set aside. Just like someone did for me. Take off your work gloves, turn off your computer, set down your cell phone, check book, dish towel; sit down for a moment and do nothing more than enjoy a piece of pie.

Pie is not bread. A good homemade pie says indulgence in a way that most common loaves of bread do not unless one is truly hungry. But a good homemade or handmade loaf of bread can also remind us of humble elements transformed: flour, salt, yeast, maybe some egg to glaze the crust. The tangible and instantaneous connection with foundational processes of life: sun ripening grain, earth and rain feeding growth, human labor and creativity transforming raw materials into life-sustaining nourishment. Attention to the ingredients connects us to a web of labor and laborers whose efforts make this food possible. We may even catch a glimpse of generations past whose ingenuity and fortitude laid the foundation for the bread before us. We could go all the way back to ancient times, but we don't have to in order to show the preciousness and perseverance of people dependent upon bread for their daily sustenance. Immigrants packed their trunks with wheat seeds when they journeyed to the great plains of North America. Refugees sewed seeds into the hems of their skirts and their children's shirts for the voyage so the new life they longed for would be sustainable in a new home. They knew that with even a bit of bread, they could be nourished. They knew they could sustain life—planting, tending, harvesting, milling, mixing, kneading, waiting, shaping, baking. Taking, giving thanks, breaking, sharing.

We meet Jesus in today's Gospel just after he has fed the multitudes. After everyone has had their fill of bread. They have had the pleasure of eating enough. We know that people have pushed away from the table Jesus set for them in the wilderness feeling sated, satisfied, because according to the story, there are even leftovers.

They ate until they were satisfied. They had enough.

Funny thing about "enough." Just what is "enough"?

The people Jesus had fed wanted a guarantee that they would always have enough. Jesus' provision of plentiful bread seemed to them something they wanted more of. So they pursue him. If they can have him, they can have bread, limitless, wonderful, unending bread. Enough.

The pursuit of a guarantee of "enough" is the stuff of which fairy tales and fables are made. Think of Midas, whose touch turns everything to gold, guaranteeing him his every desire, until his daughter runs happily into her father's embrace and becomes an immutable reminder that some things are infinitely more precious than gold. Think of the poor sailor and his wife whose magic salt mill brings them fame and fortune until, because they demand more and more, it grinds and grinds and won't stop grinding until it overflows, and drowns the sailor and his wife under an avalanche of salt and still it overflows today out through the broken windows and door of their seaside shanty and that's why the oceans are filled with salt. Think of Jesus' parable of the rich fool who spends his days pulling down his barns to build bigger ones to fill them with all his belongings, until one night the rich fool dies and finds there are no pockets in a shroud and his whole life has been consumed by the pursuit of something that ultimately leaves him empty-handed.[4]

Unfortunately, these fairy tales and fables point to a truth: it can be so hard for us to figure out what is enough, what our appetites actually are

---

4. Luke 12:13–21.

meant to lead us toward, when a craving is a clue and when it is a distraction. Dr. David Kessler, in his best-selling book, *The End of Overeating*, writes about food engineered to satisfy us momentarily but leave us wanting more and more of it. According to Dr. Kessler, food manufacturers create combinations that reinforce their product as desirable, a treat we deserve, the only thing that will satisfy—which it does, until the next time we see the ad, drive past the restaurant, get a taste for the product. Kessler describes a cycle of cue-urge-reward-habit that reinforces our body's "hunger" for unhealthy, ultimately unsatisfying food that always leaves us overfilled but unfulfilled. He quotes an advertisement from a major chain restaurant, "This isn't about grabbing a bite. It's about a bite grabbing you. 'Cause when Friday's gets hold of your appetite, we're not letting go. We are going to bring on the flavor 'til your taste buds explode like fireworks."[5] We can't say we aren't being warned.

Jesus fed hungry people. He knew people need to eat. He told his followers to feed people real, physical, tangible, nutritious food.

But he also promised that he himself would be enough. He didn't want to be just a provider of physical bread. He wants to be our bread—our sustenance, our nourishment, our daily strength, our source of satisfaction.

Jesus is bread, but he wants to fill the hunger of our hearts and not just our stomachs. He wants to fill the gnawing, aching emptiness that we try to fill with lesser things, to satisfy the longing or the boredom that we use substances of all sorts to quiet, to put an end to the grasping, fretting, worrying about having enough of anything that will in the end possess us, rather than allowing ourselves to fall into the hands of the one for whom we were made.

Jesus is daily sustenance. He is bread to be savored, gathered around. Bread to inspire thanksgiving, to remind us of the wonder of life, to strengthen us. We can contemplate him thoughtfully, chewing slowly, pondering, but we will gain more if we come to him as hungry beggars, open to whatever he places in our outstretched hands.

He was taken, blessed, and broken. He is to be shared. The sharing of his life invites us to exercise the creativity of an artisan bread-baker and the compassion of a mother sewing seeds into the clothing of her children so they will always have sustenance for the journey.

---

5. Kessler, *The End of Overeating*, 48.

Jesus said, "I am the bread of life. Whoever comes to me will never be hungry."

PROPER 15, YEAR A

Matthew 15:21–28

Jesus left that place and went away to the district of Tyre and Sidon. Just then a Canaanite woman from that region came out and started shouting, "Have mercy on me, Lord, Son of David; my daughter is tormented by a demon." But he did not answer her at all. And his disciples came and urged him, saying, "Send her away, for she keeps shouting after us." He answered, "I was sent only to the lost sheep of the house of Israel." But she came and knelt before him, saying, "Lord, help me." He answered, "It is not fair to take the children's food and throw it to the dogs." She said, "Yes, Lord, yet even the dogs eat the crumbs that fall from their masters' table." Then Jesus answered her, "Woman, great is your faith! Let it be done for you as you wish." And her daughter was healed instantly. (NRSV)

On the Border

Joseph S. Pagano

Amy and I like to travel. We love the adventure of going to new places, meeting new people, and experiencing different cultures. When I travel, there is always that moment, the moment when I cross the border, that fills me with anticipation and excitement. Crossing a bridge into Canada or going through customs at an international airport always gets me wondering about what it will be like on the other side. Will it somehow feel different to be in another country? What sights and sounds and smells will greet me? Will the air be light and crisp or soft and golden? Will the food be spicy or creamy or sweet? Will men wear neckties and hats? Will women wear long scarves and drive around in convertibles? Will mariachis play in cafes and people dance in the streets?

But crossing a border also fills me with apprehension and fear. Should I drink the water? Will they really eat horsemeat? Will packs of wild dogs nip at my pant legs? I also worry about being misunderstood. I worry that I will try to say something in French and people will stare at me or laugh at me or try to take advantage of me. I worry about taking a wrong turn and getting lost in a strange place. I wonder if people there will be friendly or unfriendly to outsiders. I also wonder how to respond if the touchy subject of politics comes up. I am fearful that my identity or the perception of my identity will evoke responses of hostility or hatred.

There is actually a new field of academic study emerging called Border Studies. It's really fascinating stuff. It began by exploring the complex political and cultural exchanges that were occurring along the U.S.-Mexico border. But Border Studies has now grown to encompass the dialogue and exchange among many different groups. Scholars are looking at the profound and transformative experiences that occur along the borderlands of culture, religion, and nationality. Individual and group identities are being reshaped and transformed. Cultures are clashing and merging. People are fighting and dancing and falling in love. In a certain sense, in our increasingly diverse world, the border has moved into our own backyards. Take a walk through a public park these days and you are likely to hear Hip Hop music, Latino music, and Caribbean music. The borderlands of language and nationality and religion can be found in almost every city and neighborhood.

In our Gospel lesson for today, we have one of the most amazing stories in all of the New Testament. It is the profound and troubling and ultimately transformative story of Jesus' encounter with the Canaanite woman. It is also a story that is situated, in almost every way, in the borderland, on the boundary between Jew and Gentile, between friend and enemy, between the sacred and the profane. It is a story of pain and power and prayer, and, ultimately, of blessing. It's not just a nice little story about Jesus granting the request of a Gentile woman. Rather, at its deepest level, it is a complex and fearful story about Jesus' own sense of identity and mission being transformed, and about the boundaries separating Jew from Gentile, friend from enemy, and male from female being transgressed. Sorry. No stories about sweet Jesus meek and mild today.

Transforming Love—Sermons for the Sundays after Pentecost

Only the fearsome blessing of God waiting for us somewhere, out there, along the borderlands of our faith.

Here's what happens. Fresh from confrontation with the religious authorities of the day, Jesus travels to the far northwest border of Israel, to the region of the cities of Tyre and Sidon. This is Gentile territory, which means that for a Jew like Jesus he was approaching enemy territory. And out there in the borderland between Jew and Gentile, between friend and enemy, Jesus is suddenly approached by a local woman. We are told that she was a Canaanite, which means she was not just any old Gentile. Canaanites were old and bitter enemies of Israel. In first century Palestine, Jesus and this woman are separated by religious boundaries, national boundaries, and gender boundaries.

The first thing that happens is that the woman starts shouting. She shouts, "Have mercy on me, Lord, Son of David; my daughter is tormented by a demon." Let's take a moment to notice some of the details because the beauty and the power of this story are found in the details. Notice that the Canaanite woman shouts to Jesus. In this shouting we see the distance between Jesus and the woman symbolized. The boundaries between Jew and Gentile, male and female, friend and enemy separate them, and, perhaps, she feels it is best not to get to close. So she shouts at him from a safe distance trying to communicate across all the boundaries that keep them separate.

Notice also that the woman says, "Have mercy on me, my daughter is tormented by a demon." She does not say have mercy on my daughter, but rather have mercy on me. Something is tormenting her daughter, and a mother who sees her daughter suffering, a mother who sees her child dying is a mother who is suffering and dying herself. The Canaanite woman herself becomes the locus, the place where the suffering of her daughter and the blessing of the Lord can meet. The pain and the power in that plea for mercy are almost too much to bear. A mother sees her child suffering and dying, and she cannot bear the pain it is causing her so she cries out, "Lord, have mercy on me because my daughter is tormented." Out in the borderlands of our faith, a woman's child is being tormented and she cries out "Lord, have mercy on me."

And, astonishingly, we are told that Jesus did not answer her, and his silence is shattering. This woman is in desperate need and in her despair she recognizes Jesus as Lord, and she cries out to him for mercy. And Jesus is silent. And just like that, we are at the mysterious borderland between heaven and earth, between the human and the divine. The Canaanite woman has come smack up against the awesome and fearful silence of God. As the Psalmist puts it, "O my God, I cry by day, but you do not answer." In the midst of the pain and the suffering in our lives we cry out to the heavens, "Lord, have mercy on us." And often times we are met with silence. The borderland between heaven and earth, between God and humanity is often experienced as a silent abyss. Out in the borderlands of our faith, we are often met with the fearful silence of God.

The question is: What will we do in the face of the mysterious silence of God? What will the Canaanite woman do in the face of this silence? Will she turn back discouraged and sorrowful? Or will she persist despite the silence of God?

She persists. Notice, the disciples say, "Send her away, for she keeps shouting after us." She keeps shouting after us. In the words of Jesus' hard-hearted disciples, we hear of the persistence of the Canaanite woman in spite of the silence of Jesus. She keeps shouting after them. She keeps crying out for mercy in spite of the silence of God. She keeps saying, "Lord, have mercy on me." When we find ourselves at the end of our rope, at the edges of our faith, we find ourselves still crying out for mercy in spite of the silence of God.

Finally, we hear from Jesus and his words are a refusal of the woman's request for mercy. He says, "I was sent only to the lost sheep of the house of Israel." It is a flat refusal. Notice also that it is a restatement of the boundary that exists between Jews and Gentiles. The Canaanite woman, a Gentile, approaches Jesus with faith, and he reminds her of the boundary that exists between them as Jew and Gentile. If she knew her history she would know that the Jewish Messiah was sent only to the lost house of Israel. He couldn't help her even if he wanted to. Case closed.

But is it really closed? Is the boundary really impossible to cross? The Canaanite woman apparently doesn't think so. So despite Jesus' reminder of the boundary that exists between them, she persists. This time she comes close and kneels down before him, as if to physically demonstrate that there doesn't need to be a boundary separating them. If Jesus will not respond to her shouts from afar, she will come close, scandalously close, she will cross the physical space that separates them, and kneel down before him and plead once more for her stricken daughter, "Lord help me."

And again Jesus rebuffs her, this time with a slur. He says, "It is not fair to take the children's food and throw it to the dogs." It is an ethnic slur that reinforces the boundary between Jew and Gentile. There is no way around it, even though many have tried to soften the words of Jesus. For Jews, dogs were unclean animals, and to refer to Gentiles as dogs was a well-known term of scorn. But he had tried silence and that didn't work. He had tried reason and that didn't work. Maybe an insult will drive her back. And as that insult crosses Jesus' lips we may find ourselves reeling backwards, wanting to retreat to the familiar territory of pious sentimentality. But what will the Canaanite woman do?

Again she persists, this time taking the insult hurled her way and turning it back upon Jesus. She will not retreat to her own territory; she will not let the barriers keep her away. Her need is too great and her faith is too strong. She says, "Yes Lord, yet even the dogs eat the crumbs that fall from their master's table." It is a clever bit of middle-eastern banter. Take the words of your opponent and throw them right back at him. Out in the borderland, the Canaanite woman takes Jesus' insult and she transforms it into a profound statement about the universal mission of Christ. Yes, Lord, seek out the lost sheep of Israel; feed the children, by all means. But remember, even the dogs, even the Gentiles, eat the crumbs that fall from the master's table.

And then something clicked and Jesus changed. His sense of identity and mission were transformed by his encounter with the Canaanite woman. Maybe he remembered the words from our Old Testament lesson, "And the foreigners who join themselves to the Lord . . . to love the name of the Lord . . . these will I bring to my holy mountain and make them joyful in my house . . . for my house shall be called a house of prayer for all peoples." Maybe Jesus realized that it was precisely because he was the Messiah of Israel that he was called to reach out to the entire world. Maybe like so much of Jesus' ministry this was the way in which God reveals his glory in the world. He understood his mission all along, but it needed to be revealed in a way people could understand. Whatever it was, something fell into place, and Jesus' sense of identity and mission was enlarged and he says, "Woman, great is your faith. Let it be done for you as you wish." And her daughter was made well.

In the messy and conflicted world of first century Palestine, Jesus encounters a Canaanite woman out on the border between Jewish and Gentile territory. It is a profound story of thresholds being crossed, boundaries being propped up and then being broken down again. It is a troubling and painful story of misunderstanding and insult. But it is also the story of a blessing received through the persistence and faith of a desperate woman. And through her persistence and faith, the walls separating Jew from Gentile, male from female, friend from enemy came tumbling down, and our understanding of Christ's mission is transformed into a message of hope and salvation for the whole world.

Where are the borderlands of your life and faith? Where have you come up against the painful reality of boundaries separating you from others, from God, even from your own self? Have you felt the pain of misunderstanding and the sting of insult that often accompanies our best efforts to get to know our neighbors? Have you come up against the fearful silence of God in the face of a cry for mercy? Our Gospel lesson for today knows of these situations in all their depth, in all their pain, and in all their confusion. And yet it also knows that when we venture out into the borderland, and when we cross the boundaries that separate us one from another we will be transformed. It may be messy. We may find our selves misunderstood and confused and insulted. But in spite of this there is a promise, a promise that at the borderlands of our faith we will be transformed, a promise that somehow as we venture out across those borders, we will find our deepest and truest selves, we will find an enlarged sense of meaning and purpose in our lives, we will find the fearsome blessing of God.

Being Like Jesus

Amy Richter

Today's Gospel lesson is a troublesome story to say the least. At first we meet a woman who has rushed out of her home to meet the man about whom she has heard so much: He has the power to cure. He has compassion for the hurting. He cares for the suffering. So, she cries out—cries of faith in what she knows to be true—"Lord! You are the Messiah! The Son of David! Have mercy on me! Please, cure my daughter!"

She is greeted by silence. Silence. From Jesus.

I wonder which is worse: silence in response to a plea for help, or a straight-forward cut to the chase response of "No, I won't help you."

At least "no" gives you something to work with, or against, or in spite of. If "no" doesn't drive you to despair, it can give you a chance to regroup, ask other people, explore other options. When Mary was about to give birth to Jesus, Joseph was told, "No, there's no room for you here in the inn. Go elsewhere." A person without health insurance can be taken from healthcare provider to healthcare provider, until finally they are given some help, even if the care they receive may not be of the highest quality, or much quality, or delivered in enough time to really help. If one food pantry has run out of food, there may be another place to turn. Maybe.

But what about when there are no other options? What about when you're already at the point of despair? What about when your only hope is in one person's ability to help, and you're greeted with silence? Silence, in response to your loudly proclaimed faith in Jesus and his ability to heal your daughter for whom you care so much. Silence is so ambiguous. It could mean no. It could mean you have wasted your breath. But it could mean maybe . . .

Then the silence is broken. By the disciples, who have their own request for Jesus. "Send her away. She keeps bothering us with her shouting and crying. Send her way." They offer no help to the woman. Just a demand, "Get rid of her. Why must the suffering make so much noise?"

Finally Jesus speaks. But his answer to the woman is "No." He breaks the ambiguity of silence by his statement that he was sent only to the lost sheep of Israel. "No," he says, "I can't help your kind." We're full up tonight. We can't accept your food stamps here. We had to make some budget cuts. I've got enough to do as it is, there are a lot of lost sheep out there.

The woman doesn't give up. She doesn't say, "Sorry to bother you. I'm sorry." Instead, she kneels before Jesus, and asks again for his help.

This time Jesus answers, "It is not fair to take the children's food and throw it to the dogs." The dogs. The dogs, he says. She was not unused to hearing her people, the Gentiles, referred to as dogs. She knew he meant her. She and her daughter: dogs. These dogs were no faithful friends. They were unclean beasts who should not be touched and who could be beaten off with sticks if necessary. Most of them, better off dead, or at least not near me. He had to say it, the disciples may be thinking. She didn't go away when he calmly explained why he couldn't help. He had to use tougher language. He didn't want to. He would rather not talk to people like that, with such harsh words. He wished she would have listened the first time.

But still she doesn't give up. She speaks again. This time she says, "Yes Lord, yet even the dogs eat the crumbs that fall from their master's table." "Okay," she says, "Okay, here's where your metaphor leads, Lord. I know you are Lord: you can still help me. Even using your metaphor, you can feed me Lord, you can make my daughter well. Feed the children, by all means, but remember, there is food, even for the dogs. Even the Gentiles eat the crumbs that fall from the masters' table."

Perhaps there was silence now too. Perhaps not. Perhaps Jesus immediately changed his mind and declared the greatness of her faith, and immediately made her daughter well, just as she wished.

Despite the good news, and there is much good news in this story, the harsh words of Jesus cannot be exegeted—interpreted—away. There is no way to soften them, although I badly want to.

"Perhaps the word should be translated 'little dog,'" say some scholars.

But to be called a small dog may be no better than to be called a dog, and a small dog may be more insignificant, more easily kicked aside.

"Perhaps Jesus was testing her faith, by using his words."

But a test of faith by calling the woman cruel names? Seeing how she responds to being degraded? To being reminded of her inferiority in the eyes of others? This makes an even less attractive picture of Jesus. And it seems an inconsistent treatment of Jesus' harsh words: when Jesus aims harsh words at Pharisees we have no trouble accepting that Jesus means them. When Jesus takes aim at a poor woman in distress, he is testing her?

"Perhaps Jesus was advocating a trickle-down theory of ministry: he ministers to the children; it's up to them to drop crumbs for the dogs."

This too fails to satisfy. Not from Jesus who otherwise ministers so completely to those he is with, who is otherwise so giving to those in need.

I cannot resolve this trouble of the text. I can't erase those words, but I can look at why, perhaps, the church chose to include this disconcerting picture of Jesus in the New Testament canon. Why, when they had so many stories to choose from, did they include this?

The reason may be in the good news it does tell. There is good news in the record of Jesus healing this girl. No longer tormented by the demon and restored to health, she and her mother can again be at peace. Jesus, Son of David, was able to heal the girl, and he did.

There is also good news in this story of the woman, who knows what she needs, wants, desires with all of her heart—enough to run and shout after the disciples and Jesus. Good news that she knows the power of Jesus to heal. Good news that she defies the customs of her society that say that only prostitutes run into the streets alone to implore men. Good news that she keeps shouting, and replying to Jesus.

There is more good news: that she defies more social norms and says that, yes, she wants her daughter to be healed. Her daughter, who is not a son in a society where sons are more valuable, less of an economic burden, more important, and perhaps more worth saving. And our New Testament Gospel text says, yes, this is good news: that the Canaanite woman interceded on behalf of her daughter.

And there is still more good news: the woman ministers to Jesus. Her response results in his change of mind. He says, "Great is your faith. Let it be done." She believes and proclaims and speaks with Jesus, and he decides to heal her daughter. Whatever the reason for his initial responses to the woman, his final response comes when he sees the situation differently. Jesus again becomes the agent of God's redeeming presence. Jesus heals. Their ministry is interactive. They minister to each other, the woman and Jesus. And this, says our Gospel, is good news.

Maybe here at last is a story where we can be like Jesus, where we can be as much like Jesus as we are like the rebuking and mistaken disciples; as much like Jesus as we are like the distraught woman looking for our own healing, or healing for someone we love. We are always supposed to strive to be like Jesus, but perhaps here is a place where we may have a little more connection. Jesus appears to have changed his mind, to have broadened his vision, to have increased his willingness to help others, to have learned. Isn't that part of what life is about? To take that risk? To learn how we can do ministry together. To interact with people and the Gospel story and Jesus Christ in such a way that we might even arrive at a new vision. Maybe here, we can be like Jesus, who changes his mind, and decides to heal after all. Maybe we can. Maybe we can be like Jesus if we keep this story in mind, and consider that maybe really to have a change of mind and heart that results in good news for ourselves and others takes hard work, and honest, faithful interaction with other people, just like in our story this morning.

A Man, A Woman, A Word of Love

PROPER 25, YEAR B

Mark 9:30–37

Jesus and his disciples went on from there and passed through Galilee. He did not want anyone to know it; for he was teaching his disciples, saying to them, "The Son of Man is to be betrayed into human hands, and they will kill him, and three days after being killed, he will rise again." But they did not understand what he was saying and were afraid to ask him.

Then they came to Capernaum; and when he was in the house he asked them, "What were you arguing about on the way?" But they were silent, for on the way they had argued with one another who was the greatest. He sat down, called the twelve, and said to them, "Whoever wants to be first must be last of all and servant of all." Then he took a little child and put it among them; and taking it in his arms, he said to them, "Whoever welcomes one such child in my name welcomes me, and whoever welcomes me welcomes not me but the one who sent me." (NRSV)

We're Number One

Amy Richter with Joseph Pagano

When I was serving a parish in Chicago, Joe and I participated in a 10-mile race in a suburb called Forest Park. After the 10-mile run was over, a second race was held, this one for children. The course was about two blocks long. Parents and other spectators lined up on either side of the street. The starting gun sounded and people broke out into wild cheers as little children came running down the street as fast as they could toward the finish line. One little girl was speeding along. Running quickly and confidently, she was making great time toward the finish line.

As she came down the block I noticed that she was wearing the number one on her race bib. Well, no wonder, I thought. The low numbers usually go to people who have won in the past and to those who sign up early. No wonder she is number one. Soon after her, a couple of boys came along, running very fast. But I noticed that they too were wearing the number one. More and more children came past, and now we were into the part of the group that weren't speedy or certain. Some looked unsure about which way to head or why they were doing this. All were wearing number one.

The race directors had done a very nice thing: every child was wearing the same number, the number that tends to mark importance and accomplishment, all were number one in that event, whether they broke the ribbon at the finish line or had to be coaxed by a parent into heading the right direction, or carried across the finish line. Number one.

I think that's the way God sees us too. We're all number one in God's eyes, all loved with the same abundant, no-strings attached, crazy, irrepressible love. All of us.

I don't know why that can be so hard for us to understand or accept—why humans persist in treating love, even God's love, as something that may run out, something we have to earn, qualify for, or mete out on God's behalf like we're measuring sugar into a teacup, rather than staring at a big ocean full of love, and God keeps calling out to us, come on in, the water's great!

The disciples certainly struggled to understand the nature of God's love. Here it is manifest before them in the person and love of Jesus, and they still don't get it. He has just told them that he loves them so much that he is willing to die for them—that he will die for them, and rise again. He has been teaching them about the boundless, unending love of God that manifests itself in lives of service to others. But on the way home, they start comparing credentials.

"Well, I must be the greatest—I've given up so much."

"You know he called me first, I must be the greatest."

"I had a great career going until Jesus called me, I must be the greatest..."

"I'm number one."

"No, I am."

"Nuh uh. I'm number one."

"So, guys, what are you talking about?" asks Jesus.

"Uh ... nothing."

Jesus sits down and says, "Whoever wants to be first must be last of all and servant of all." Jesus isn't just playing with words—he really wants the disciples to get the picture, so he gives them an image. Jesus takes a child in his arms and says, "This is what I am talking about. This is what the Gospel, this good news I'm living is all about: Whoever welcomes someone like this in my name welcomes me."

The disciples' eyebrows go up. Peter shrugs, palms up. John looks at James and mouths, "Really?" This is Jesus' example of whom we are to serve and how we are to act? This child is the very opposite of influence. A child pays no taxes, has no resumé, has no physical strength, can earn nothing; and, in Jesus' time especially, was society's very definition of insignificance.

In Jesus' time, children were not viewed with sentimentality. We still do not do right by children today—we are still willing to let children in this world go hungry, go without proper medical attention, struggle through an inadequate education. But at least we talk better about children. We describe them as innocent, trusting, delightful, valuable, full of potential and promise.

Not so in Jesus' day. Children were the least, the unimportant, the marginal. They are completely dependent on those around them; they are vulnerable and weak; they need help; they are not self-sufficient. This child, says Jesus, is the model disciple in the kingdom of God.

See the picture? The child has nothing; but wrapped up in Jesus' arms, the child has everything. Jesus is saying, like a child, allow yourself to be dependent on God. Jesus says, if you truly open yourself to the grace of the kingdom and stand before Christ as open to possibility as a child, if you come before God with the fervency of a toddler who wants nothing other than to be held, if you bring nothing with you besides your emptiness and your need, then something amazing will take place inside of you. You will actually become more open and more free. You will become a lot less concerned about protecting your position in the world. You'll feel sillier and sillier about building your life around what others think and whether they think you're the greatest. You will spend more and more time trying to understand others and their needs and how to reach out to them, without thinking what you might get in return. You will want to be part of a community that embraces weakness, even when it's your weakness, and knows that there is more than enough love to go around for everyone everywhere.

Here is a story Joe tells about his interaction with some children God put in his midst:

Transforming Love—Sermons for the Sundays after Pentecost

One of the most memorable sermons I ever preached was a children's sermon. I cannot remember now what the topic of the sermon was. In any event, I had prepared what I thought was a wonderful children's sermon talking about the lessons, relating to children's lives, time for children's reflections, maybe a craft. Great stuff. Well, I started into my homily and was immediately interrupted by a little boy who held up an arm with a plaster cast on it. I stopped and said, "Yes, Johnny, do you want to share something?"

"I broke my arm."

"Oh, I'm so sorry to hear that," I said, "it must have hurt, how long will you have the cast on?" and all those things you talk about. Then, I return to my prepared sermon on whatever the topic was, and then a little girl put up her hand. I stopped and called on her, and she said, "You know, one time, I broke my finger, and I had to wear a splint for four weeks." And I said, "Oh I'm sorry to hear that sweetheart, that must have hurt, and is your finger okay now?" and it was, and then I tried to return to my sermon.

Now lots of hands had gone up, and everyone had a story about some injury they had sustained at some point.

"I banged my head and had to get stitches."

"I fell down and cut my knees."

And we even widened the circle to include stories about brothers or sisters or other kids they knew who had broken collar bones and had wisdom teeth pulled or sustained other bangs and bruises. By this time I had not gotten through any of my sermon, so I decided there was only one thing left to do. I rolled up my pant leg, and showed them the scar from my ACL surgery, the old kind that leaves a huge zipper down the front of your knee. And they were really impressed. I told them I had to wear a cast for six weeks and had to walk on crutches. And then a sort of reverent silence came over us, and we all shared a moment, I like to think, reflecting on how our common vulnerabilities had formed us into a community of the wounded. There we were sitting on the floor bound together by our common humanity and our human weakness, and I felt the presence and peace of Christ. It may have been the best sermon I ever preached.

I want to be a great rector. I want St. Anne's to be a great parish. But I want us to be great in the only way that matters: with Jesus' kingdom greatness—greatness that comes from embracing our dependency on Jesus Christ and following his footsteps, pouring ourselves out in love and service for others, shaping our life as a community in a cross-shaped way—offering prayer and praise to God and loving service toward others.

I want this to be a place where we treasure the children and youth among us as disciples of Jesus Christ—now—not as future disciples, but as full participants in Christ's body. I want this to be a place where those who teach children and lead children, where parents who do the hard work of bringing their children to worship and education, have their ministries of teaching and leading and bringing honored. I want this to be a church community where when people see us they say, See how they love one another.

May the greatness of Jesus be the only greatness we seek.

PROPER 25, YEAR C

Luke 18:9–14

Jesus told this parable to some who trusted in themselves that they were righteous and regarded others with contempt: "Two men went up to the temple to pray, one a Pharisee and the other a tax collector. The Pharisee, standing by himself, was praying thus, 'God, I thank you that I am not like other people: thieves, rogues, adulterers, or even like this tax collector. I fast twice a week; I give a tenth of all my income.' But the tax collector, standing far off, would not even look up to heaven, but was beating his breast and saying, 'God, be merciful to me, a sinner!' I tell you, this man went down to his home justified rather than the other; for all who exalt themselves will be humbled, but all who humble themselves will be exalted." (NRSV)

Do You Love Me?

Joseph Pagano with Amy Richter

Every person who is born into this world has one basic question that underlies his or her whole life: "Do you love me?" Everyone, who lives and learns and grows, who works and worships and plays, who grays and grows old and dies, keeps asking, over and over, this fundamental question: "Do you love me?"

We humans are created for connection: connection with others, connection with the universe, and connection with God. Being hardwired for relationship, we seek communion and reconciliation with all people, with the cosmos, and with God. This desire is the search for love, and the state of being in which all are united in love with one another and with God, we call heaven. All of human life is a quest for love.

Unfortunately, the fundamental question "Do you love me?" is soon transformed by genetics, by socialization, by sin, by whatever, into a different question, "Am I worthy to be loved?" or even more tragically, "What can I do to be worthy of your love?"

With these distorted questions the unfortunate soul seizes upon the answers provided by family or society or even the church: I will be rich, I will be famous, I will be powerful, I will be successful, I will be elected, I will be esteemed, I will be holy, I will be ordained. In the process, we manage to convince ourselves that we will be happy if we achieve these goals, and by happy we mean that we will be loved. The funny and the sad thing is that we continue to persist in these delusions even after experience repeatedly has shown them to be false. Maybe the next promotion or the next home or the next prize will bring true happiness. Throughout our lives, we continue to make the same mistake of trying to find in the finite and limited things of the world the response that is found only in the true object of our desire, in the God of love. Tragically we make idols of our strength, our money, our success, and our power. Perhaps most tragically we make idols of our religion. We latch on to the things that should be pointing us to God and make them into idols.

In our Gospel lesson for today, we hear the Parable of the Pharisee and the Tax Collector. In the form of a parable, Jesus presents the central theological teaching of God's justification of sinners and the ultimate futility of self-righteousness. Two men, one a Pharisee and the other a tax collector, go up to the temple to pray. The Pharisee stands by himself and he really is quite impressive. Although centuries of Christian interpretation have led us to think of Pharisees as the bad guys, this is not fair. They are often presented as Jesus' opponents in the Gospels, but we need to remember that they were society's good people. They were dependable, honest, upright, good neighbors, contributors to the community. Quite frankly, they were the type of folks we would all like to have as members of our parishes. The Pharisee is a man at home in the temple. He says his prayers. He gives more than he has to. Although the tithe on income was standard, he tithes on everything he has, and many people would have benefited from his generosity. He stands in the correct posture for prayer in the temple, arms raised and head lifted. But—and this is an important but—in his prayer, he has nothing to ask of God. He's basically giving God a progress report. As far as he can tell, he's got it all under control, and he's happy about it: "God I thank you that I am not like other people: thieves, unrighteous folks, adulterers, or even like that tax collector over there."

Meanwhile, standing off at a distance, is the tax collector. He has got nothing to show for himself and he knows it. He earned his living by working for a foreign government collecting taxes from his own people. For years he has collected high taxes from his Jewish neighbors to give to the Roman government. He gives the Romans their flat rate on every head, and makes his money by charging an excess and keeping it for himself. Basically, he is a crook, a traitor, and a lowlife. He is guilty and he knows it. He keeps his head lowered as he comes into the temple. We don't know why his guilt has got the better of him today, but there he is in the temple, full of remorse, beating his breast and saying, "God be merciful to me a sinner." He doesn't even promise to shape up. All he does is ask for God's mercy.

The surprise ending of the story is that the Pharisee, who gives a wonderful performance in the temple, goes home empty. He came asking nothing of God and he goes home getting nothing from God. The tax collector, despicable fellow that he is, shows up empty handed asking for God's mercy, and goes home justified, that is, in right relationship with God.

We may hear this parable as a lesson on humility: don't be proud like the Pharisee. Go home and be humble like the tax collector. And just like that, we fall into a trap. We take a parable about God's amazing, unconditional grace and acceptance, and turn it into a story about how we can earn or merit God's love. We've got the answer now. If we can just be humble like the tax collector and not be puffed up with pride like the Pharisee, then God will accept us and love us. We may even find ourselves praying, "God, I thank thee that I am not like the Pharisee."

The trap here is that we ask the wrong question of this parable. It's that distorted question, what can I do to be worthy of your love? The Pharisee in the parable asks this question, and he thinks he has the answer in his religious observance. He fasts, he prays, he tithes, he lives an upright life. The tragedy and the irony is that in the very act of demonstrating that he is worthy of love, he is cutting himself off from his neighbors and from God. The tragedy and the irony of trying to make ourselves worthy of love through our supposed virtues, even the virtue of humility, is that we end up casting a sideward glance at others and measuring ourselves against them. If I need to earn God's love, then I will have to be better than the other guy. In the fire of God's love even our supposed virtues need to be burned away.

But if we ask the right question, the question, do you love me? then the parable gives us an answer. To the question, do you love me? God replies resoundingly and forever, "Yes." The tax collector's humility was not a virtue that earns him God's love and acceptance. The tax collector's humility is a posture of openness in which he is able to receive God's love.

Ultimately, the Pharisee and the tax collector are the same. They both need God's love. The difference is that the Pharisee doesn't know it and the tax collector does. The tax collector goes up to the temple with nothing to show for himself. His hands and his heart are empty and he knows it, and therefore he has room to experience the gospel, the good news that there is nothing we need to do, nothing we can do to earn the grace and love of God.

I remember the moment when I realized Amy loved me unconditionally. It was early on in our relationship. It was freeing. It was a gift. Lord knows it was not because of my good looks, brilliance, or wit. I'm bald, need to plod my way through things, and tell corny jokes. And miracle of miracles, or grace upon grace, she still loves me and still laughs at my jokes. But, in all seriousness, to know that I am loved no matter what, for better for worse, for richer for poorer, in sickness and in health, is one of the greatest gifts I have ever received. It has also allowed me to grow in ways I think God would have me to grow. Knowing that I am loved and in turn giving myself away in love for my wife has enabled me to become more fully the person God created me to be. Knowing that I am loved has enabled me to reach out in love and concern for others, to develop my capacities for generosity, compassion, to forgive and to allow myself to be forgiven. That is why I think of marriage as a sacrament. It is a concrete, personal, intimate way in which I have known the grace and mercy of God. Knowing the unconditional love of my wife is one very real way I know the unconditional love of God.

A Man, A Woman, A Word of Love

The love that moves the sun and the other stars, the love that creates, sustains, and redeems the cosmos, is always uttering its eternal "Yes" to our question "Do you love me?" The only thing we need to do is open ourselves to that love and return it. Everything else is a veil before our eyes, thrown up by our culture, our career, and our churches. All self-flattery and self-importance and self-righteousness ends in futility. When we stop reciting our resumes in the temple, the incarnate love of God meets us and embraces us, saying I know your pain, my beloved, and I forgive your sins. I know your emptiness and I will fill it and I will fill you with my melting love.

Bibliography

Alighieri, Dante. *Paradiso*. Translated by Mark Musa. New York: Penguin, 1986.

_____. *Purgatorio*. Translated by Mark Musa. New York: Penguin, 1985.

Aria, Barbara. "How to Say No (Without Saying No)." No pages. Online: http://www.redbookmag.com/kids-family/advice/how-to-say-no.

Austin, Alfred. *Savonarola: A Tragedy*. London: MacMillan and Co., 1881.

Brooks, Phillips. *Sermons for the principal festivals and fasts of the church year*. New York: E. P. Dutton and Company, 1895.

Browning, Don S. *The Moral Context of Pastoral Care*. Philadelphia: Westminster, 1976.

Brussat, Frederic and Mary Ann Brussat. *Spiritual Literacy: Reading the Sacred in Everyday Life*. New York: Touchstone, 1996.

Cardenal, Ernesto. *To Live is to Love: Meditations on Love and Spirituality*. New York: Doubleday, 1972.

Crossan, John Dominic. "Appendix: Bodily-Resurrection Faith." In Robert B. Stewart, *The Resurrection of Jesus*, edited by Robert B. Stewart, 171–86. Minneapolis: Augsburg Fortress, 2006.

Gardner, W. H., and N. H. MacKenzie, editors. *The Poems of Gerard Manley Hopkins*. Oxford: Oxford University Press, 1967.

Basser, Herbert W. "A Love for All Seasons: Weeping in Jewish Sources." In *Holy Tears: Weeping in the Religious Imagination*, edited by Kimberley Christine Patton and John Stratton Hawley, 178–200. Princeton: Princeton University Press, 2005.

Bietoletti, S. et al., *Florence: Art and Architecture*. English edition. Potsdam, Germany: h. f. ullmann, 2007.

Dittenberger, W. *Orientis Graeci Inscriptiones Selectai*. 2 vols. Leipzig: Hirzel, 1903–05.

Ehrenberg, Victor, and Arnold H. M. Jones, *Documents Illustrating the Reigns of Augustus and Tiberius*. Oxford: Clarendon Press, 1949.

Foreman, Judy. "Why Cry?" *The Boston Globe* (March 8, 2010), G8.

Foster, Richard. *Celebration of Discipline: the Path to Spiritual Growth*, 3rd ed. New York: HarperCollins, 1998.

Foster, Thomas C. *How to Read Literature Like a Professor*. New York: HarperCollins, 2003.

Fowler, James W. *Stages of Faith: The Psychology of Human Development and the Quest for Meaning*. San Francisco: Harper & Row, 1981.

Frost, David. "An Interview with Maya Angelou." WNET/Channel 13, 1995. No pages. Online: www.newsun.com/angelou.html.

Hollinghurst, Alan. *The Line of Beauty*. New York: Bloomsbury, 2004.

Holmgren, Stephen. *Ethics After Easter*. Church's New Teaching Series 9. Cambridge, MA: Cowley Publications, 2000.

Bibliography

James, Henry. "The High Bid." In *The Complete Plays of Henry James*, edited by Leon Edel, 555–603. New York: Oxford University Press, 1990.

H. W. Janson, *History of Art: a Survey of the Major Visual Arts from the Dawn of History to the Present Day*. 2nd ed. New York: Harry N. Abrams, 1984.

Kahn, Albert E. *Joys and Sorrows: Reflections by Pablo Casals*. New York: Simon & Schuster, 1970.

Kessler, David A. *The End of Overeating: Taking Control of the Insatiable American Appetite*. New York: Rodale, 2009.

Mangione, Jerre and Ben Morreale. *La Storia: Five Centuries of the Italian American Experience*. New York: HarperCollins, 1992.

Martin, Douglas. "Giorgio Carbone, Elected Prince of Seborga, Dies at 73." In *The New York Times* (December 13, 2009), A47.

Meeks, Wayne A. "Social Functions of Apocalyptic Language in Pauline Christianity." In *Apocalypticism in the Mediterranean World and the Near East: Proceedings of the International Colloquium on Apocalypticism, Uppsala, August 12–17, 1979*, edited by David Hellhom, 687–705. Tübingen: Mohr-Siebeck, 1982.

Parker, Bettsee. "'Send Thou Me'": God's Weeping and the Sanctification of Ground Zero." In *Holy Tears: Weeping in the Religious Imagination*, edited by Kimberley Christine Patton and John Stratton Hawley, 274–99. Princeton: Princeton University Press, 2005.

Patton, Kimberley Christine and John Stratton Hawley. "Introduction." In *Holy Tears: Weeping in the Religious Imagination*, edited by Kimberley Christine Patton and John Stratton Hawley, 1-23. Princeton: Princeton University Press, 2005.

Paulsell, Stephanie. *Honoring the Body: Meditations on a Christian Practice*. San Francisco: Jossey-Bass, 2002.

Polen, Nehemia. "'Sealing the Book with Tears': Divine Weeping on Mount Nebo and in the Warsaw Ghetto." In *Holy Tears: Weeping in the Religious Imagination*, edited by Kimberley Christine Patton and John Stratton Hawley, 83–93. Princeton: Princeton University Press, 2005.

Schmidt, Richard H. "Christmas: Let Me Hold You, Dear Little Jesus." *Episcopal Life*, December, 1994.

Shakespeare, William. *The Riverside Shakespeare*, 2nd ed., edited by G. Blakemore Evans. New York: Houghton Mifflin, 1997.

Tutu, Desmond. *No Future Without Forgiveness*. New York: Doubleday, 1999.

Wallis, Jim. *God's Politics: A New Vision for Faith and Politics in America*. San Francisco: HarperCollins, 2005.

Wright, N. T. and John Dominic Crossan. "The Resurrection: Historical Event or Theological Explanation? A Dialogue." In Robert B. Stewart, *The Resurrection of Jesus: John Dominic Crossan and N. T. Wright in Dialogue*, edited by Robert B. Stewart, 16–47. Minneapolis: Augsburg Fortress, 2006.

Wright, N.T. *Simply Christian*. New York: Harpers, 2006.

www.ingramcontent.com/pod-product-compliance
Lightning Source LLC
Chambersburg PA
CBHW071623170426
43195CB00038B/2088